ANTIQUE AIRPLANES

ANTIQUE AIRPLANES

CHRIS SORENSEN

AND THE EDITORS OF *Flying Magazine*

Photographs by Chris Sorensen

CHARLES SCRIBNER'S SONS/NEW YORK

Copyright © 1979 Ziff-Davis Publishing Company

Library of Congress Cataloging in Publication Data

Sorensen, Chris.
  Antique airplanes.

  Bibliography: p.
  Includes index.
  1. Airplanes—Collectors and collecting.
2. Airplanes—Restoration. I. Flying. II. Title.
TL506.AlS67   629.133′34′075   78-11272
ISBN 0-684-15817-5

Portions of this book are based on material
originally published in *Aeroplane Monthly* and
Shell Aviation News. Information on airplane
museums originally appeared in *Aircraft Museum
Directory*.

1 3 5 7 9 11 13 15 17 19   M/D/C   20 18 16 14 12 10 8 6 4 2

Printed in the United States of America

CONTENTS

PREFACE

We at *Flying* Magazine emphasize aviation as it is now, covering new developments in aircraft and equipment design as best we can, but we have a soft spot in our hearts for old airplanes, the wonderful antiques that are the subject of this book. As we celebrate our fiftieth anniversary as a publication, it is only fitting that we pay homage not only to vintage flying machines but to the many across our nation who give their energy, money, and time to preserve those airplanes against the erosions of time.

In putting together this book, we have learned much about the antique movement and its people. The movement itself is robust and growing, thank goodness, and its people come across as amazingly talented, imaginative, and tenacious. They are good craftsmen, and they are good pilots. In many ways, they represent the best qualities among aviators, not the least of which is generosity. They have given freely of their knowledge and cooperation in helping us with our research.

We are particularly grateful to Chris Sorensen for his excellent work. He has pursued the task with the tenacity and creativity worthy of a first-rate antiquer. We should also point out that every photograph in this book was taken by him. In addition, he made most of the black-and-white prints and edited all the photos used in the book.

We appreciate greatly the contributions of writers such as Peter Garrison, Norbert Slepyan, and Peter Lert. The vital work of preparing the manuscript was performed by Jo Cavallo, Dorothy Scheuer, and Geraldine Ivins. The executive editor of the project was Norbert Slepyan.

A special word of thanks is due our editor at Scribners, Laurie Graham, whose high standards as a bookperson have been excellent guides to us magazine people in creating this book.

ROBERT B. PARKE
Publisher, *Flying* Magazine

FOREWORD
What Is an Antique Airplane?

The definition of an antique airplane varies with different organizations.

As far as the Federal Aviation Administration (FAA) is concerned, any aircraft that is more than thirty years old is an antique. The significance of this to an antique restorer is that he may place the registration numbers of his craft on their original location—the wings. All modern aircraft are currently required by the FAA to exhibit the numbers on the fuselage, although there has been some discussion about returning to wing placement.

Not only may the antiquer put the numbers in their rightful place; he may also use the old designation "NC" in front of them instead of just "N," adding a final touch of authenticity.*

The Experimental Aircraft Association (EAA), which has Vintage and Classic divisions, defines an antique as any aircraft manufactured before January 1, 1942. The EAA Classic Period includes those aircraft built between the beginning of 1946 and the end of 1950.

Neither the FAA nor the EAA definition of an antique aircraft satisfied the members of the Antique Aircraft Association (AAA), who felt that two distinctly different aviation eras and aircraft were being lumped together: those built between 1919 and 1935, and those built from the end of 1936 through 1942. Also included are post–World War II aircraft manufactured under Approved Type Certificates issued before World War II.

In order to distinguish between these eras and aircraft types (mainly to clarify competition rules), the AAA held two standards meetings, where they established separate categories for vintage aircraft.

The first category, the Pioneer Period, included aircraft from 1903 to 1914 or the beginning of World War I. The World War I Period

*This change in regulations was brought about primarily by the efforts of Robert L. Taylor, president of the Antique Airplane Association.

covers the planes built between 1914 and 1919, when virtually every aircraft was of military design, such as the Standard J-1, and Curtiss JN-4.

There were few aircraft built in the years 1919 and 1920. Most of the planes flying were designed as three-place, open-cockpit, OX-5–powered biplanes. The OX-5 biplanes were all conceived along the lines of the Jenny and the Standard.

The Antique Period covers the years 1920 through 1936. During the first part of this period, public confidence in aviation was at an all-time low, and airplanes were treated as a curiosity. Recognition of and confidence in aircraft as a reliable mode of transportation began when Lindbergh flew the Atlantic in 1927. The early Ryans, Travel Airs, Fokkers, and Fords of the 1920s and 1930s, with their closed cabins, were the first attempts to make the airplane a practical method of transportation. Finally, in about 1934–35, fast and comfortable light-planes, such as the Cessna Airmaster, Staggerwing Beech, and Stinson Reliant, made aircraft an attractive mode of transport for individual owners.

The AAA states that an airplane is an antique if it was built before 1935 or if the government issued an Approved Type Certificate (ATC) for it before 1935. Thus a Stearman PT-17 built in 1942 would still qualify as an antique because its ATC was granted in 1934.

The AAA's Classic Period, from 1935 to 1941, is the era antiquers refer to as the golden age of lightplanes, because so much significant development took place in such a short time. Not only were many outstanding closed-cockpit designs produced, but they also featured comfortable, spacious, and relatively soundproof interiors. Aircraft speeds approached or surpassed 200 mph, and more sophisticated radio navigation equipment began to be developed.

Certain aircraft built between 1942 and 1945 are termed War Birds, a limited number of rare flying machines built between 1946 and 1950 are designated Neoclassics, and everything manufactured after that is simply a modern airplane. An antiquer might conceivably submit the following definition for a modern aircraft: a transportation device employed in the search for antiques.

For the novice, finding a vintage airplane is largely a matter of luck. If, however, you have already decided on the type of antique (Stearman, Waco, Monocoupe, etc.) you would like to own, there is a more logical procedure.

The Antique Aircraft Association can tell you whether there is a type club for the particular plane you want. If not, you can at least obtain the names and addresses of other owners. Talking with club members or owners who share the same strong interest in a special type can lead the prospective buyer to an old airplane hidden away in a dark corner of a hangar, or to a curious-looking relic tucked in the back of a barn.

Whether you are set on a particular type of antique or just shopping around, another good source is *Trade-A-Plane.* This publication lists individual for-sale ads, as well as auctions of plane collections and estate sales.

In addition, as good a place as any to start must be a small, grassy airport with a few old buildings and not too much activity. Here one is likely to find a half-dozen friendly souls sitting around talking or simply passing the time of day. Falling into conversation with them could provide a lead. Perhaps one of them has a friend who has heard of an old airplane up at Smithville, or another might suggest that a fellow down the road knows somebody who is into that sort of thing. It's up to you to decide how vigorously you want to pursue these leads—most of which will lead nowhere. But it's a way to start and it will put you in touch with some fascinating people.

More experienced antique hunters often have a host of leads they mean to follow up as time allows; when you meet these people, they will occasionally pass one on to you that might lead to a strike. The point to remember is that, as in so many other things, persistence pays off. One day you will find yourself helping someone tug open an old hangar door; and there in the shadows you'll see a dust-covered relic of a bygone era that you know will be *your* antique.

A "buddy ride." One of the antiquer's favorite activities is to take friends up for a ride, particularly if the friend happens to own the same type of aircraft. Here George Hefflinger (right) tries out the Hayes Waco. Hefflinger also owns a beautiful Cabin Waco.

INTRODUCTION
The Spell of the Antique

Antique airplanes are barely antique in the normal sense of the word; the oldest are three score and ten. Buildings, furniture, or paintings of such an age might be considered modern. But the chronology of aviation is compressed; fifty years of aviation are like five hundred years of architecture; seventy years are millennia. The science of flight has been carried along on an accelerating wave of technological progress that today has reached such a dizzying pace that in the time between conception and manufacture a new invention may, paradoxically, become obsolete.

Looking back at the airplanes of fifty years ago we are looking, in aeronautical terms, into another world. It is as if a historian could visit a Roman city, speak with its inhabitants, shop in its markets, and sweat in its baths. That world of the childhood of aviation was one of eccentric individuals, of precarious enterprises, of daring guesses and sometimes spectacular risks. It was, compared to ours, a dark age in which ignorance laid traps everywhere for the unlucky or incautious. All that has changed now. Aeronautics is not an extremely subtle science, and the technique of building ordinary private passenger aircraft is now so well known, has become so quotidian and mundane, that a hobbyist can instruct himself in it and design and build an airplane with a good likelihood of equaling or surpassing commercial products.

So much the more remarkable, then, that sixty years ago a person who set out to build an airplane was traveling into terra incognita. He was an explorer, visiting places where few or none had been before, where the land was not tamed and no one knew what beast or hostile native lurked. Air was an inhospitable medium; engines were unreliable, structures uncertain, materials untested. The dynamics of flight were beginning to be well enough understood, but the refinements of stability and control that make the modern airplane comfortable and easy to fly were barely guessed at.

The airplanes built in the period before the institutionalization of design were idiosyncratic, imaginative creations. They had a touch of artistry about them, which is difficult to find in airplanes designed by committees and computers. They were not ideal airplanes; in the light of current knowledge, almost everything was wrong with them.

Inadequately powered by overweight engines, they depended on huge wings for support. Their structures were often flimsy and excessively flexible; their controls sometimes worked topsy-turvy—right aileron making the nose swing wildly to the left—or, at certain speeds, not at all; and if they had the bad luck to stall or enter a spin, they usually could not recover. Brakeless, they bounced and jolted to uncertain stops on fields of mud, ditches, and sod, and often finished ingloriously upended. The record of their misfortunes was inscribed upon them in scars of fabric tape and sutures of baling wire.

Although the "modern" tricycle landing gear was experimented with very early on, most airplanes built before World War II had tailwheel gear, because it was better suited to landing on the rough, unpaved fields of that era, particularly if they happened to be emergency fields originally intended for farm crops. But the tailwheel gear was also an invention of the devil, sometimes monstrously difficult to control, which made landing some designs much harder than flying them and sent many a pilot careening off the runway into a fence in payment for the slightest inattention.

But, unlike today's airplanes, the old ones had looks and personalities as distinct from one another as those of human individuals. They were like people in many ways—each with its own face, way of movement, responsiveness, kindness or cruelty, balkiness or docility. Even among the individuals of a series, as among brothers and sisters, there were differences. With the mechanization of manufacture and the standardization of materials, techniques, and styles, those particularities were erased, and the airplane with an individual personality became a thing of the past.

That singularity—even among members of a superficially similar series—is at the heart of the antique airplane's charm. There were few of them to begin with, each different from the others, and most have decayed or been lost or destroyed, so those that remain are unique treasures, like very old persons who remember historic wars of their childhood.

The criteria for a noteworthy antique center on its uniqueness and individuality. In cases where the type of airplane still survives in large numbers—though most of these are "classic" rather than antique—it is the fidelity and care of the restoration that attracts admiration. Ideally, however, an antique should be of a type virtually extinct; it should reproduce the original in every detail; it should be of impeccable finish and craftsmanship throughout; and it should radiate the personality that sets it apart from other airplanes.

The careful craftsmanship lavished upon antiques is not an attempt to duplicate the condition of the airplane when it was new. No airplane that was built to work, rather than be looked at, ever had the polished brass fittings, the deep hand-rubbed paints, the fancy upholstery, the sparkling engine of the prize-winning antique of today. They were plainer then, splattered with oil and mud, scraped and faded after a few months in the field, tarnished and patched so soon that their builders would no more have thought to embellish them with spit and polish than a farmer would his tractor. The embellishments of the present-day restorers are their way of paying tribute to the airplanes and to themselves. They are also a defiance of aging. The chrome, the layers of paint, the varnish and polish are a way of crystalizing, making permanent, something that has barely escaped the grip of age and decay.

At work here too is an age-old, genuinely primitive impulse—that of decoration. The antiquer shares with the antique auto buff, with certain modelers and Stone Age tribesmen, a fascination with the embellishment of simple things. He falls in love with the luster of paints, the velvety glow of wood, the brilliance of brass and chrome. If there is a special charm to the shape of a rocker arm on an engine, how much more so when the part has been polished so that it seems to move with the movements of your eye even when it is standing still.

To appreciate the nature of the work, you must have seen how a restoration begins and how it ends. There is much personal taste involved: many decisions must be taken as to what will be allowed to pass, what will be discarded, what repaired, and what replaced. There

Old parts can be used as patterns for new. Duane Golding holds the old seats in his hands, one as it was and the other flattened out so that he could cut the new metal for the seats you see installed in the fuselage. On the floor are the two old floorboards that were used to make the replacements, also in the fuselage.

must be a certain homogeneity throughout the restoration. If a few parts are left damaged, corroded, or dirty, they pollute the airplane (if only in the mind of the owner, since much can be hidden under new fabric). Old airplanes are complicated things; the stamp-and-rivet simplicity of the modern had not yet come into being. Even the metal ones were assembled from a superfluity of parts, joined together with an extravagant indifference to hours of labor. Labor was cheap then, and the tireless devotion of the restorer answers nicely to the airplane's insatiable appetite for human effort.

Sometimes a restorer will begin with what he thinks will be a re-cover and repaint job, but when he has removed the old fabric he finds rotten ribs, rusted steel, dented tubing. He repairs these, always feeling, in a borderline case, that he "might as well" do such-and-such too, since it isn't *quite* perfect. The more parts that have been done anew, the more glaring are the remaining imperfections of the old. In the end everything comes apart, everything is sandblasted, primed, varnished, sanded, shined. In a careful restoration, parts shine even in the darkness, eternally out of sight.

Once one is committed to a certain level of perfection, it is very difficult to accept parts that fall short. Because of this refusal to compromise, certain projects seem to take forever and to cost a fortune. However, not all restorers are so fanatical; many are satisfied to bring an airplane back to clean working condition—that in which it originally operated. If the original engine is not available, they are satisfied to substitute another one, a modern one if need be, as well disguised as necessary. It is enough for them to perpetuate the airplane, without monumentalizing it. They find sufficient satisfaction in flying an airplane that is unusual, that attracts attention, and that sets them apart from the majority of airport arrivals and departures. Performance has in most cases nothing to do with it, since antique and classic airplanes are not, generally speaking, sparkling performers—a few famous exceptions like the Beech Staggerwing merely proving the rule. The sensations of flying some of the old airplanes are not always pleasing, either. Slow to respond and difficult to land, they're not all great fun by any means. What is seductive about owning them is their appearance and ambience. There is the feeling, as you bask in the rays of the setting sun on a Sunday afternoon, that time has stopped and that old airplanes and pilots will never cease to fly.

L. W. Lindemer of Circle Pines, Minnesota, fuels his 1944 Beech D-17S Staggerwing during the Blakesburg fly-in.

A lonely Stinson awaits the loving hand of an antiquer to restore it to its former glory. This one was behind a row of hangars at Dacy Airport in Harvard, Illinois.

PILOT: LOUISE PFOUTZ
WEST ALEX.OHIO

The fun of flying an old airplane is not limited by gender. Louise Pfoutz is one of several dyed-in-the-wool lady antiquers. She flies a BT-13, a 4,496-pound aircraft at gross. Her husband flies an identical model with a different paint scheme. They and their two aircraft are Blakesburg regulars.

Part of it may be nostalgia, that currently fashionable sentiment to which so many features of our culture are attributed; but nostalgia implies that the sufferer remembers the time for which he longs and therefore that all antiquers are old men. Some are (though few are as old as certain antique airplanes), but many are young, and their fascination with the airplanes of the past arises not from a longing to recapture the smells and sounds of their youth but from a sensitivity to a style of beauty which, like that of the stately automobiles of the teens and twenties, is gone forever.*

Old airplanes are like unusual clothing. No one gets particular pleasure out of appearing in run-of-the-mill mass-produced clothing, but one's vanity is piqued by the unusual outfit that draws admiring attention. The airplane is like a suit of tasteful clothing; it clothes the ego of the pilot, giving him a mask with which he replaces himself, and so is lifted above the common run of men and held up to general admiration.

There are also other, less egotistical reasons for loving antique airplanes. Some people are reluctant to let the past die; like art collectors, they treasure the beautiful things of other years and eras. Many old airplanes qualify amply as works of art. They express the taste of the maker as surely as a painting does. Their proportions and shapes are haunting, characteristic, and elegant; the quaint guesses at streamlining that formed them reflect the hands of primitive masters. There is a bravery about them that we cannot allow to perish. And so the rotting hulks in hangars and barns wait only for the person who is moved by their plight. A rotting airplane has the same pathetic quality as a dead bird—its one-time freedom and exuberance contrast so sharply with its present downfall. To bring the dead back to life and to save the moribund are acts of compassion, and addicts of old airplanes feel such compassion strongly.

The airplanes that can qualify as antiques exist already; the best the aircraft industry has been able to do since 1935 is to generate a few classics—a very few. We are dealing here with a vanishing species, with creatures under the threat of extinction, and with people whose love for the noble relics of the past makes them move heaven and earth to save them. Many airplanes have already been restored to pristine condition; many more remain, waiting to be discovered by someone who will fix them up. Whatever it is that inspires antiquers—whether pity, nostalgia, or vanity—it continues to manifest itself in a movement that grows every year in size and enthusiasm. There is a good chance for every decaying antique that someone, someday, will turn up to save it.

*The antique movement is composed of people of *all* ages. In fact, efforts are made to ensure that fly-ins have appeal to all family members, and new young blood is strongly encouraged to become part of the movement. *Both* sexes are welcome.

I

AIRPLANES AND THEIR PEOPLE

Harold Neumann points out the small, battery-powered radio he uses only infrequently and then with great reluctance. He takes it out when he does aerobatics.

1

A Case of "Monomania"

Many antiquers recreate airplanes in order to live a past they didn't have, to transport themselves back in time, to savor—like the historian or the art connoisseur—not only the artifact but the spirit of the age in which it was created. Not Harold Neumann. At age seventy, he has recreated something he *has* had and for a time did without.

The artifact is a 1941 Monocoupe, a wily, beautiful white machine that was rescued from oblivion when Neumann found it, rotting and forgotten. He had been looking for any Monocoupe so that he could pick up where he had left off when, in 1936, he joined what was then Transcontinental and Western Airlines and had become Trans World Airlines when he retired from line service in 1966. There had been a Monocoupe in his youth; he had flown it and a successor as a barn-stormer and air racer. He had grazed the pylons in the Gordon Bennett air races. Then he had gone on to fly DC-3s, Constellations, 707 jets, and other behemoths that are to a small-plane pilot what buses are to sports-car lovers.

On retiring back to his farm near Kansas City, Harold Neumann, a lover of flight and machines, wanted what he'd left behind. For most people, such a wish would be followed by a sighed admission that you can't go home again. For Neumann, the wish was father to the search.

Neumann is the nation's oldest active aerobatic competitor, a twister and turner of airplanes, continually renewing his symbiotic relationship with old aircraft and at the same time teaching younger pilots how to beat him at his own aeronautical game.

That game started in 1926, 30,000 hours' worth of flying ago. When the fabled Benny Howard was building airplanes in Moline, Illinois, young Harold Neumann would wait at the airport for Howard—then flying for United Air Lines—to bring in the mail. The young, eager Neumann talked Howard into letting him get the tightness out of his racers. It was a practice at Moline to let people build up time in Monocoupes when it was necessary for someone to loosen up the controls prior to certification by the Department of Commerce. In time, Neumann was flying in the Gordon Bennett races, and in 1935 he won the Thompson Trophy while flying the legendary DGA-6 *Mister Mulligan*. This airplane is to air racing what a blower Bentley is to auto racing. The very name inspires affection. It was inspired by the swift and popular Monocoupe 90-series design.

Neumann joined the airlines because he wanted to see the world. For thirty years he flew the world of ranges and bearings and omnis, a world of electronic wonders and often of sheer boredom. Yet he is a man who loves to fly alone, virtually sprawled out in the cockpit of an airplane that, when well trimmed, will fly itself. He doesn't like to fly on instruments. On the line, he always flew by instrument rules—the government said he had to. Now, he doesn't want any part of it.

Begrudgingly, he has installed a portable, standby-type radio, powered by a motorcycle battery. "All I want is something to call the tower with when I get there, so I can land legally." Neumann has captained the most sophisticated airliners into the most high-level international airports in the land, but now he wants little from the aeronautical powers that be. If he doesn't have the right frequency, he will patiently circle and circle until someone takes out a light gun and flashes it green for him to land. Some hard words and veiled threats may follow—this 30,000-hour aviator is an anachronism in The System.

The System wasn't built for Monocoupes, and Neumann was glad to leave it. Once he had his Monocoupe again, rescued from a pasture in Reynolds, Ohio, in 1967, he was on his way to happiness. Part of that happiness was due to the fact that, though the airframe of the Monocoupe was in less than pristine condition, the engine was a 145-horsepower Warner—just what Neumann wanted.

Neumann got a friend, Eddie Fisher, who had helped to build the original Howard racers, including *Mister Mulligan*, to help with the restoration work. This partnership was a clear case of what Kurt Vonnegut would call a *karass,* a collection of people and objects that belong together forever. Neumann may have had such an awareness as he pondered upon a name for his Monocoupe.

In his background lay years of racing Howards when they were bright with newness and nowness. Here was a Monocoupe, rebuilt with much help by a crew led by Eddie Fisher. Here was a big-engined, small-tailed, V-strutted wonder with a paint scheme differing from that of *Mister Mulligan* only in that the trim set against the dominant white was blue rather than gold. "I thought about it and looked at it," Neumann says, "and it looked light, fast, and flighty." Like *Mister Mulligan.* "So I decided, why, hell, this is my little *Mulligan.*" Painted neatly on the cowl is the airplane's moniker, *Little Mulligan.*

When Harold Neumann lands *Little Mulligan* at its home, Johnson County Airport, just outside Kansas City, it is as though the 1930s were returning. But it is more than that. This airplane, which, like so many ships of that period, looks like a small airframe screwed onto a big engine, is a working machine and a peculiar product of its owner's passion for tinkering, for optimizing what such a machine will do, for doing the unorthodox. That's why you will see him landing it and taxiing with the door four inches open. "During the taxi, you have to snake around so you don't run into anything. I leave the door open about four inches to see better. I can keep it open with my knee. It gives my knee more room and makes it easier to operate the heel brakes."

Harold Neumann wipes down *Little Mulligan.* Note the self-adjusting Aeromatic prop.

You will also see him landing without flaps, although the airplane has them. "I never cared for flaps," he says. "At certain times, on a wet field or on grass, for example, flaps allow you to lift off a little more quickly, but I don't like the feel of an airplane with flaps. When you use them, everything is very mechanical. You just come down with a little higher approach and squat in. Without flaps, you can feel the airflow and play around with the wing to get the airplane to do what you want. That's what I enjoy."

The visibility in his Monocoupe can be a real problem, what with that big Warner up front in that huge, round cowling. A right crosswind can play havoc with an approach.

The 90-series Monocoupe design was the inspiration for Benny Howard's DGA-6. The Howard racers had about the same wingspan as the 90-series Monocoupes.* They also had a larger fuselage and tail—they looked better for that, too—and developed 550 horsepower at 2200 rpm on 87-octane fuel, using a Pratt & Whitney Wasp engine.**

Neumann's Monocoupe was originally a 90AF, since it was first delivered with a Franklin engine. To listen to Neumann provide an exegesis on the evolution of the 90 series is like listening to a paleontologist describe how the prehistoric *eohippus* became the modern horse.

The 145-hp Warner appeared on the 110 Special (the clipped-wing version of the 90) and the D-145 model, which was slightly bigger than the 90 series. The 90 series began with the 90-hp Lambert R-266 and was subsequently fitted with the 90-hp Warner Scarab, Jr., the 90-hp Franklin 4AC-199, the 100-hp Franklin 4A4-100, and the 115-hp Lycoming 0-235C1. Some owners have modified their 145-hp Warners to produce 165 horsepower, but you can't really install a 165 on the 145 mount. You have to put 165 heads on the 145 and then make up some manifolds to fit in the 145, which in turn involves making changes in the cowling.

Eighty-octane fuel has of late become very difficult for many pilots to obtain, for reasons that are complicated and—some oil companies say—compelling. Whatever the reasons, old airplanes, such as *Little Mulligan* and far more recent aircraft, including most of the airplanes used for training today, are perforce being run on 100-octane avgas,

---

*The DGA-6 had a 31-foot, 8-inch wingspan, and the 90-series Monocoupe had a 32-foot wingspan.
**For the 1935 Thompson Trophy race, this engine was rated at 830 hp on 100-octane fuel for a maximum speed of 287 mph and a rate of climb of 4450 fpm!

which can foul sparkplugs if not carefully watched. The Monocoupe has an apparent advantage, however, for its low-compression engine apparently resists the effects of a higher octane fuel. It's a matter of keeping the plugs and breaker points clean and set, says Neumann.

Neumann's Monocoupe is noteworthy for other reasons: it has a self-adjusting Aeromatic prop, which Neumann contends is good for aerobatic flying. With it, he says, "you can dive the plane, open the throttle, and let her go."

In its heyday the Monocoupe was a hot rod. Even today, it serves well as an aerobatic machine. Part of Neumann's routine is a hammerhead, a move in which the airplane climbs as nearly vertically as it can. In time, the momentum runs out, and the wings stall. The pilot kicks some rudder and brings the airplane over into a dive. When performed well, the hammerhead is a beautifully graceful maneuver, a kind of aerial sigh, an ethereal gesture in which both machine and pilot seem to accept, reluctantly, the power of gravity. In the cockpit, maintaining that kind of gracefulness is tough, but "the Monocoupe really hangs in there," says Neumann. You must be careful that the plane doesn't fly out of or slide back from its position during the crucial pivot. For an older airplane, the Monocoupe hammerheads with charm.

Neumann competes in the Sportsman's category, which has the least complicated maneuvers. His routine includes a loop, an Immelmann, a half-loop with a half-rollout, a split S, a hammerhead, and a snap roll. The snap roll is especially difficult, for the Monocoupe likes to climb and the nose gets too high before it breaks. During a contest, Neumann will pull four and a half to five positive Gs, holding onto the stick with both hands. The Monocoupe will run well inverted, but Neumann dislikes such flying. He's happy to leave the more complicated and free-wheeling routines to "the younger boys." But what maneuvers he does, he does in what is perhaps one of the best machines for aerobatics designed in the thirties. The Monocoupe has a Clark-Y airfoil, which, although not a symmetrical airfoil, does the job well enough. At Oshkosh, Wisconsin, in 1975, Neumann competed against fifty other pilots and placed eighth. That's against the best. Occasionally he places first, as in a recent contest at Olathe, Kansas. His desire is simply to be a good contender, to be interested and participating. He won't, however, burn out an engine practicing, nor will he burn himself out with an intense determination to succeed.

The first step in bailing out of his Monocoupe would be for Neumann to lift up on this handle, which takes the pins out of the door hinges. Next he would pull the door latch, the door would fall off, and he would roll out of the cockpit and hit the silk.

His passion for tinkering shows up in small but readily visible ways. Even as he talks with a visitor, he reveals his true love in the way he moves, swiftly, nervously about his airplane. Mustachioed, peering through eyeglasses slightly reminiscent of Groucho Marx, he tinkers here and tinkers there, checking on some new refinement to the *Little Mulligan.*

The Rube Goldberg cliché doesn't really apply here—quite the opposite. Goldberg's inventions were based on doing simple things in complicated ways. That sort of thing doesn't go in aviation. For instance, if you have to bail out of your airplane in a hurry, you need a simple way of getting out. That's just what Neumann has provided for his Monocoupe. He describes his method of exiting in a dead mono-tone. The listener may be imagining the original crunch of metal that can announce a structural failure, or the sudden absence of roaring that proclaims the demise of an engine, and he may be feeling the wrench-ing of his body as the airplane heads downward, perhaps at a very unusual attitude. Neumann would, of course, perceive those things, too, but he would also have his mind just where it ought to be—on the escape procedure he has provided for himself. "First, I would unbuckle the shoulder harness and then the two seatbelt straps," he says, as if describing how he would climb off one of the combines on his farm. Then he would pull up on a handle, removing the two door hinge pins. One final door latch at the rear would be released, and out he would go. The escape would be quite rapid.

He has also solved the problem that vexes many aerobatic pilots— keeping the engine going in inverted flight. Some engines and their support systems (particularly the lubrication system) are constructed to stay alive when upside down, but most aren't, and those that aren't may go quiet within less than a minute of inversion. Neumann has installed a "flop line" in the right wing tank. The line is weighted so that it falls to the part of the tank that becomes the bottom when the Monocoupe is upside down. Neumann also has added an extra fuel pump for his aerobatic work, a device that has proved invaluable in forestalling airlocks.

Perhaps the most curious addition Neumann has made is a starting device that seems terribly wacky, until the logic of the thing comes through. The *Little Mulligan* has no electric starter, so it must be propped. It usually has no copilot, so Neumann must swing the prop himself and then get into the cockpit in time to switch on the extra pump, which is located next to the wing root. Not getting the pump on in time means an unstarted engine. Leaving the pump on before propping could mean flooding.

The answer to the problem was to find a way to get the engine to do what Neumann wasn't fast enough to do: get the extra pump on once the powerplant had caught. He bent a piece of copper tubing into the shape of a U, then attached the U to the toggle switch of the pump with a small piece of rubber hose. The clevis curves around the top of the door frame and can be positioned so that it rests against the window of the right door. Neumann leaves the door ajar—it is the trigger of the mechanism.

Making sure the airplane is securely chocked—many an airplane has proceeded pilotless, on its own, once the engine has started—he prop-starts the engine. The first blast of propwash slams the door shut, pushing on the copper tube and switching on the pump. Almost casually, Neumann can enter his airplane as the engine warms.

Other pilots might have taken the still simpler course of installing an electric starter, but Neumann wants to keep the weight down in his aerobatic airplane. Far better, in his view, to use some ingenuity.

At least once, however, his ingenuity did him wrong. The ceiling of the Monocoupe's cockpit is a skylight of blue-tinted plastic, which is

The switch for *Little Mulligan*'s extra fuel pump is turned on when the prop blast pushes the door shut and shoves the copper tubing U in and up. The tubing can be seen looping around under the words *Fuel pump* in the upper left hand corner of the picture.

excellent for visibility but an instant heater on sunny days. No problem: Neumann installed a regular spring-loaded roll-up window shade, which can be pulled forward and attached up front with a small chain-and-hook arrangement.

It all worked fine until one day in 1967, when he was flying with his wife, Inez, and found himself in a terrible storm. A fast-moving front had developed that any forecaster would have said wasn't supposed to be there, and it caught Neumann. He went low, thinking he could get to some thin spots that seemed to be beckoning. He had seen early morning showers take on a frightening aspect before. But this was no garden variety early morning shower.

The treetops were just below his wheels as he tried to thread his way out of the gathering gloom. The roiling air began to toss the plane about, just about the time that Ms. Neumann decided to roll back the skylight curtain. But the curtain wouldn't roll back up.

"Here she was," Neumann describes it, "holding onto the curtain, trying to keep it off my head. There I was, trying to fly the airplane in this terrific wind and rain and at the same time trying to make a turn to get back out of it." They made it, and Neumann took the spring out of the curtain, but Ms. Neumann never forgot the incident.

To make matters worse, on that same trip, as they were heading home, the engine seized. Suddenly, there they were at 4,000 feet, with the prop resting motionless in front of them, not even windmilling. Neumann would have to dead-stick the airplane in. Spotting an alfalfa field, he aimed for it, moving the stick diligently, which meant that his wife's legs took a beating in the cramped cockpit. They landed safely— no damage to machine or personnel; but such a trip was enough for her. She had flown with her husband constantly during the 1930s (they were married in 1929) and was completely familiar with light-airplane aviation, but she has since taken almost exclusively to airliners.

Neumann doesn't mind flying alone. "I get up there and follow a railroad or a big highway and just take it easy. I stretch my legs out onto the other side of the cockpit, and I may have a hold of the stick and I may not. I just go sailing along, enjoying every minute of it."

It's been a long road from the Gordon Bennett races, the Thompson Trophy, and the hard days of airline pioneering, and Neumann has learned well how to pace himself, to get his priorities straight. As an aerobatic contender, he wants to be good, to be in there, a factor, but he

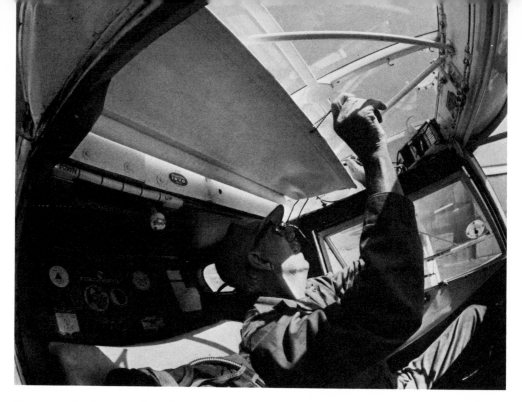

Neumann demonstrates how the curtain can be drawn across the "skylight" of his cockpit. It was a handy device until one day . . .

is not about to burn himself out so that the fun goes out of it. As a flyer and a contest judge he has become more and more of a teacher, challenged and beaten by young people he has helped. That's okay by him.

The Monocoupe is a fine airplane for an active flyer. Once squared away in level flight, it flies itself, hands off. When it was designed, the government insisted that airplanes be able to find their own level with the pilot's hands and feet off the controls. Utmost stability was essential. The Monocoupe was such an airplane. Its wings are long, its ailerons are heavy, but it is stable.

Neumann's passion for fashioning innovations for his airplane has extended to his setting a piece of masking tape at a 45-degree angle to the wing chord in the middle of the window on each door. He uses the tape as a horizon reference line. In one maneuver, he rolls inverted, flies straight and level, then pulls into a 45-degree inverted climb, lining the tapes with the horizon to achieve the proper angle.

One hears a lot these days about professional pilots who become jaded about flying, about airline pilots who are content to be aerial bus drivers—just get it up there, turn on the autopilot, and collect your pay. In any profession, mediocrity can combine with routine to create boredom. However, pilots like Harold Neumann give the lie to the idea that constant flying can dull one's attachment to it. For him, the challenge is always what it was in the beginning: how to be master of the airplane. "The way to do that," he says, "is to get up high and find out what the airplane can do. Aerobatics takes the unknown quantity out of an airplane."

Neumann moves easily about his farm and its old machines, the feed grinder, the corn plucker, the combines, and says with pride about these agricultural jalopies, "That's history." Well, *he* is fifty years of flying history and more years than that of rootedness to the heartland of America. He talks of having an antique sale and giving his stuff away, and he talks of selling his 315 acres—in one parcel, no divvying up the land, no way—but one wonders, for his pride is still strong as he talks about his land and about the hardships of farming. It is also strong when he talks about the fly-ins he hosts, gatherings of as many as thirty-eight airplanes, at his own little airstrip—if you're going to land there, keep in mind the hollow at the middle and the fact that the runway isn't level. He talks about selling these things. He talks about it. There's one thing he doesn't talk about selling: *Little Mulligan.*

Harold Neumann at the gate to his 315-acre farm.

The Howard DGA-15P is an engine with an airplane attached. The big Pratt & Whitney dominates the aircraft from almost any angle. The polished pushrod tubes and the bulbous spinner are the visual trademarks of this powerplant. To hear one first gurgle, then purr to life with a deep, throaty roar is one of the sweetest sounds in aviation.

2

Friends Ship

Damned Good Airplane—that's what the brilliant designer Benjamin O. Howard planned it to be, and a damned good airplane it was, so that's what he called it (abbreviated to DGA). As we have seen, the famous racing plane *Mister Mulligan,* which was flown by Harold Neumann in the thirties, was a DGA-6. It was the only airplane to win the 300-mile, closed-course Thompson Trophy race *and* the transcontinental Bendix Trophy race from Los Angeles to Cleveland, taking both of them in 1935.

The Howard DGAs were actually inspired by the Monocoupe, which Benny Howard first flew in 1931. Looking ahead to the emergence of a fast, cross-country executive transport, Howard replaced the Monocoupe's 90-hp Lambert engine with a Pratt & Whitney Wasp that developed 550 hp but was boosted to 830 hp for racing. It was a big airplane, with a fuselage as wide as its radial engine, and it was unusual for a racer in that it had a spacious cabin with side-by-side seating and dual controls.

Howard then proceeded to produce five commercial versions of the -6: the DGA-8, -9, -11, -12, and -15. The DGA-15, produced from 1940 to 1944, was the biggest, with a larger tail group and a wider fuselage. It was also a bit slower than the others and carried a 450-hp Pratt & Whitney R-985 Wasp Junior engine.

An airplane with a pedigree like that is bound to have a good reputation, one would think, and for the most part that principle applies to the DGA. But there's one problem, so the conventional wisdom goes: though it is a kitten in the air, the DGA is a tiger on the ground. To hear the stories, you'd think the airplane had a mania for ground-looping—and John Turgyan, a thirty-six-year-old airline pilot from Trenton, New Jersey, heard a lot of those tales. One nickname he heard for the DGA-15P he was contemplating buying was *The Ensign Eliminator*, because, in use as an instrument trainer by the navy, it ground-looped so often with young officers at the controls.

His friends seemed sure he'd kill himself in the Howard if he bought it. He remained adamant. "The more I heard about a Howard, the more I wanted one," he relates. "How do you explain a thing like that—except suicidal tendencies?" He still can't explain, even after five years of ownership, why he first wanted it so much. His most vivid experience with a Howard up to that time had been during his days as a line boy at Robbinsville-Trenton Airport, in New Jersey, when a How-

The Howard in flight.

ard's tailwheel rolled over his foot. That was 300 pounds' worth of agony.

The reason seems tied to Turgyan's basic love for airplanes of the golden age, the Staggerwings, Spartans, and other machines of that era and quality. He is sure that the conditions under which such classy ships could be designed and built are gone forever. Furthermore, he is addicted to taildraggers. Virtually all his flight time, except for his airline work, has been in taildraggers. When he was nineteen, he acquired a Piper J-3. He kept it for two years, then sold it to buy a Ryan PT-22, a very strong and challenging trainer used in World War II. He has also owned a Tri-Champ and a Stinson 108-3 Station Wagon.

Turgyan loves fly-ins and air shows, and at the 1970 Antique Airplane Association fly-in in Ottumwa, Iowa,* he saw the Howard he wanted, a gorgeous DGA-15P. The money side of such a purchase didn't bother him. Single, with few outside responsibilities, he is very much a now person. Sounding like a Schlitz beer slogan, he says, "You're only going to live once. If you've got it, you do it. If you don't have it, you can't do it." But the owner didn't want to sell.

There ensued two days of fierce campaigning by Turgyan. Melting the owner's heart with booze was out—he didn't drink. Melting his soul with money also seemed hopeless. "Name your price," Turgyan would say. "You'll never get another chance like this again." At last, the man consented—to be paid a price that was unheard of at the time. Turgyan won't say what it was, but that fiscal enormity has been surpassed by the present value of his Howard.

With this go-ahead, Turgyan unleashed a small whirlwind of wheeling and dealing at Ottumwa. He closed the deal on the Howard, then turned around and sold his Stinson, whose new owner immediately sold his J-3 Cub. Three airplanes had been bought and sold in sixty seconds.

At first, ownership of the Howard brought a shock. Turgyan loved its slick look, but he'd had no experience with big radial-engined airplanes. "When I was trying to buy the Howard, I paced the floor at night saying, 'What am I going to do? What am I going to do?' After I bought it, I paced the floor at night saying, 'What did I do? What did I do?'"

*The AAA held its first fly-ins at Ottumwa, then later at Blakesburg, a few miles away.

What he'd done was to consign himself to five years of remaking the Howard, bit by bit, slowly perfecting it, correcting things that were not quite up to snuff.

The Howard's logbooks showed that thrice in its life the airplane had met with minor violence. It had been ground-looped twice while being used by the navy, necessitating replacement of the left wing, gear, and belly skins. After its release from service in 1945, it was flown for some 200 hours and again ground-looped. This time the right gear and belly skins were replaced.

With his friends' warnings about the Howard still ringing in his ears, Turgyan became acquainted with his new airplane. He was delighted to be able to climb to 9,500 feet, trim the airplane, and just sit back and relax while it virtually flew itself. However, he was also to learn that you can't take the Howard for granted, especially while landing. He's never ground-looped it, but he's learned that the airplane has another little trick with which to impress the unwary. "It can get you to make a fool out of yourself—one time before ten thousand people."

It happened first at a gathering at Blakesburg, Iowa, in 1974. He took some friends up for a ride. Darkness began setting in as he prepared to land, dulling the visual cues. The Howard has very springy landing gear. The heavy coil springs on each side of the gear were designed on the soft side to provide a smoother ride over rough runways and taxiways. Turgyan set up the airplane just as he wanted it for a greaser with which to impress his passengers. But in the dusky light he misjudged his height as he flared, for suddenly the ground was *there* and the Howard was bouncing twenty feet high. In such a case, the prescribed procedure is to go around and try to get the redness out of your cheeks. The next touchdown was good. He's been embarrassed that way only a few times, but he stays wary. "It doesn't take a Superman to fly it," he says, "but it's no J-3, either."

The perfecting of the airplane has been easily as important as the flying of it—and Turgyan flies it a lot, some seven hundred hours in the past five years. Also in that time he has gradually rebuilt every system and component, learning tinsmithing on his own to do the work. The interior of the Howard has taken on new elegance since Turgyan refurbished it with leather.

He has also made his Howard into an excellent instrument airplane. To get the optimum transportation value, the plane must have a strong IFR* capability, for here is an airplane that can carry 150 gallons of fuel for a 1,200-mile range that puts Kansas City within nonstop reach from Trenton. Nor is making it to Florida a big deal—as long as he can deal with the weather going IFR. Turgyan has installed dual 360 coms, dual nav receivers, dual glideslopes, an ADF marker beacon, transponder, DME, and encoding altimeter. He's also planning on RNAV. There is bound to be criticism from antique purists about destroying the authenticity of the restoration, but Turgyan points out that his airplane had originally been built as an instrument trainer for the navy and that when it emerged from the factory it was loaded with radios. He's merely updating those radios.

He flies IFR for at least 70 percent of the trips he makes. He'd prefer not to and would rather climb to 10,500 feet and just pick up a heading, but flying in the East means weather flying. The Howard was designed to be strong, and its high wing loading and comparatively short wingspan provide the needed strength for coping with turbulence and carrying light ice. So well was the airplane designed by Benny Howard that there has never been an Airworthiness Directive issued for it. Few airplanes designed more recently have that kind of record.

The most difficult thing about flying the Howard IFR is that Air Traffic Control gets confused about him. A typical exchange with ATC might be:

TURGYAN—New York Center, this is Howard November Charlie 95462 with you at ten thousand.

CENTER—Roger, 95462.—Say type aircraft again? And was that November *Charlie?*

TURGYAN—Roger, I'm a Howard and Charlie stands for commercial.

Like as not the controller, who may not even have been born when this DGA was rolled out of the factory, then receives some dubious help from a self-styled aviation historian in the tower. "Probably a Howard five hundred," the "historian" might say, referring to a veteran twin-

---

*Instrument *F*light *R*ules, one of the two sets of regulations under which pilots must fly, the other being Visual Flight Rules (VFR). In the latter, a pilot gains course information from such visual cues as the natural horizon, but when these cues do not exist, as in clouds or rain, he must fly IFR, using instruments as his guides.

John Turgyan carefully removes some of the speed ring sheet metal. According to him, the metal "never fit just exactly right." Coming from this master restorer, that remark means that the fit was a fraction of an inch off here and there. This kind of attention to detail has won Turgyan over sixty trophies, an outstanding reputation in the antique movement, and, most important, the respect and admiration of his friends. His insight into what it takes to do a good job of restoration has prompted his selection by the EAA's Antique and Classic Division to be one of its judges at Oshkosh year after year. This picture also shows a solution to Turgyan's shop-lighting problem. The stand on the right is basically a length of tubing fitted to a steel wheel that is mounted on casters. A few standard electrical outlets were added.

The cockpit of John Turgyan's Howard DGA-15P. The panel has been extensively reworked during the installation of modern radio gear. The "sunken" look and the slanted surface at the bottom of the panel are unique to Howards, many of which (including this one) were used by the navy as instrument trainers. The interior has been completely redone and is an exceptionally neat and aesthetically harmonious job. It features brown leather on the seats and side panels, a beige headliner, and leather-covered control yokes with very precise stitching in the seams. The aircraft has IFR capability.

engine transport that flies much faster than the DGA.* Airplanes like Turgyan's are anomalies in the modern world. The C isn't used on registration numbers anymore. So the ritual of explanation goes on virtually every time Turgyan switches frequencies, which on a long IFR trip can be often.

The Howard was meant to be a junior airliner when it was first conceived, and it has that sort of feel. The controls are a bit heavy and the airplane is very stable. The Howard cruises nicely at a 170-mph true airspeed. At two and a half tons and carrying only a thirty-eight-foot wingspan, the airplane exhibits fantastic short-field performance. Turgyan is confident that he can operate it out of a fifteen-hundred-foot strip at maximum gross weight. "The climb is spectacular. It will outclimb anything in its class. A conservative estimate would be an average of fifteen hundred feet per minute." The Howard stalls at fifty-nine mph and does so cleanly, with rudder and aileron control available right through the stall.

Just looking at the Howard, with its big Pratt & Whitney up front, tells you that it is inherently nose-heavy, which means that the center of gravity is a matter of key concern during loading. Turgyan is well aware that many Howards have been put onto their noses when landed with a forward CG by a pilot eager to slam on the brakes, something he has never personally experienced.

John Turgyan says his Howard has changed his life, has given him new direction, and attracted new friends. He has friends in every state. His medium is fly-ins, which have taken on a new richness for him.

"At first, I'd work my butt off getting the airplane in shape for an air show, cleaning and waxing it. It was fun and satisfying when I won some recognition for that. And I enjoyed flying to the air shows. Then, as time went on, I realized that the most important thing is the people involved. There's a deep-rooted camaraderie in the antique movement.

*The confusion revolves around the Lockheed Lodestar modification by Dee Howard called the Howard 500, an aircraft that became a reasonably popular—and very fast—executive transport.

OPPOSITE
The Howard in a turn. This aircraft has high wing loading on a wing that has practically no dihedral. The bit of fabric trailing from the left hand bracing wire attached to the stabilizing surfaces indicates registration at a fly-in.

It's like being part of one big family. We all know what's involved in owning and restoring an antique plane. There's a special respect you develop for your fellow antiquers."

He has won sixty trophies with the Howard but is no longer so interested in the recognition aspect of the movement. He flies when and where he wants, free now of ambitions for trophies. What he treasures are his friendships. He used to carry a toolbox with him when he flew, but no more. "No matter when I might get stuck, there's an antiquer who will lend me his toolbox." He tells of the time at Blakesburg when an Aeronca was blown over in a storm. In a day, unbeknownst to the owner, enough money was collected to get the airplane rebuilt. "You don't see generosity like that at the *average* airport." He plans to fly the perimeter of the United States, stopping in every state along the way to visit friends.

TLC: It is probable that few inanimate things in the world receive more attention than antique airplanes. Is that a smile on the face of this Howard?

John Turgyan brings his Howard to Blakesburg, for an Antique Airplane Association fly-in.

The Howard that will carry him has had twelve civilian owners in its time, not including Turgyan, but few could have appreciated it as well. Few could have worked on detail after detail to bring the airplane, as he says, "up to snuff." He figures that two-thirds of his life is spent at the airport. There are few Howards on the antique show circuit, so Turgyan's DGA-15P is something special. He has since replaced it with the only other remaining DGA-11 Howard, so the process will begin anew. The restoring and displaying will offer him great gratification, though now not nearly so much as the knowledge that when he lands at an air show there will be good friends there. There is also the good feeling of knowing that, as one elderly spectator, a stranger, told him, "Mister, when you come in with an airplane like this, you haven't just landed, you have *arrived.*"

3

A Family Affair

Loving teamwork goes far in aviation. It often is as good as money and can certainly do worlds for the health of an airplane.

Wayne and Marie Hayes, of Yardville, New Jersey, own a 1937 Cabin Waco, one of twelve S-7 Standard Cabin Wacos still flying out of the 932 originally built. It was completed on April 27, 1937, designated as a YKS-7. Its registration then was NC17701. It still is.

The Cabin Wacos were interesting airplanes in their own time, for they flourished when manufacturers of civilian aircraft had all but given up on big-engined biplanes. A new generation of low-powered, relatively inexpensive monoplanes was in the ascendant in the early 1930s. Except for the Beech Model 17 Staggerwing, a classic in itself, the Cabin Wacos were unique as a flourishing line of closed-cockpit biplanes. Furthermore, the basic design of these machines was a departure, for the Wacos were actually what has been called two-winged monoplanes, that is, the upper longerons were attached to the upper wing. A further refinement was the use of strut bracing, which had previously been used only on monoplanes. The Waco was roomy as virtually no biplane had been, and the cockpit was closed, a mark of how general aviation was beginning to leave the helmet-and-goggles era.

OPPOSITE

The Hayes Waco in the sunset. Note the beautiful finish on the wings, the radical outward lean of the N struts between the wings, and the rod in the foreground that connects the upper and lower ailerons. Double ailerons are more often a characteristic of biplanes built for aerobatics than for cross-country work. This feature, which gives the aircraft a quicker roll rate and more positive bank control response, is one of several built into the Waco, resulting in outstanding flying characteristics and making it a popular restoration choice.

So the Hayes's airplane is a milestone of sorts, well worth keeping healthy. Besides, in spite of its slightly stubby look, it has a rounded grace that is a welcome relief from the angular, squared-off airplanes that now dominate the general-aviation fleet. Red with white trim, it looks as if a whole collection of French curves had gone into the design of its fuselage, stabilizer, wings, and wheelpants. To see it flying over the Jersey shore brings back an entire era, as if it were flying to Lakehurst to watch a Zeppelin make its run in from Europe. It looks like the toy of a millionaire playboy.

That wouldn't be far from the truth, either. In the heyday of Hollywood, stars such as Wallace Beery and Edgar Bergen owned Cabin Wacos, as did movie studios, oil companies, including Texaco, Standard, and Shell—and an aerial hero, Wiley Post. One of the best-known Cabin Wacos was the 1939 ARE photo ship used by New York's picture newspaper, the *Daily News*. It is still flying, in the hands of a private owner.

Wayne Hayes is no millionaire, and anything but a playboy. He is an industrious steelworker who has been with U.S. Steel for twenty-four years. Sometimes he works nights, from 4:00 P.M. to midnight, or, even more grueling, from midnight to eight in the morning. He also has a part-time job at a gas station—all in the service of his wife, his home, and his Waco.

Marie Hayes does not have a salaried job—her work is more important than merely bringing in a paycheck. While Wayne is at the steel mill or gas station, Marie may be handling inquiries from other Waco owners, preparing her home for the next influx of visiting antiquers—they're a highly sociable bunch—feeding antiquers who may have delayed their departure, or giving the airplane a rubdown. A great deal of the airplane's warm glow is the result of her compounding, cleaning, wet-sanding, and polishing.

For most pilots, a Sunday afternoon ride in the family airplane begins with a simple preflight and perhaps cleaning the windshield and wiping a few bugs from the wings. If the Hayes family had felt that way about airplanes, they might just as well have owned a 1970s-vintage Piper, Beech, or Cessna. For Wayne Hayes, "Owning, maintaining, and flying this mechanical monster is a joy we both share. It is our toy, savings account, sweat, and tears, and we love it."

When Sunday rolls around, there they are at Trenton-Robbinsville Airport, with Ms. Hayes polishing the airplane to perfection and her

The Waco's polished aluminum prop has airfoil all the way to its center. This feature ostensibly helps to cool the Jacobs radial.

husband wiping the engine down. When they finally get the power-plant started, it is smooth and confident in the manner of a fine-tuned Swiss watch.

The Hayes family is part of that legion of fly-in fanatics who make general aviation, and in particular antiquing, a communal affair. Marie and Wayne go to virtually every gathering of the faithful that is accessible to them. Their year-round zeal comes with a certain amount of discomfort, which might have dampened their enthusiasm for cabin biplanes. This 1937 machine is drafty in winter and hot in summer. Long flights can be wearing, even boring; but for the Hayeses the glow has never worn off. This Waco has known a great many long flights since its first year.

Its logbooks recall that the aircraft was first owned by H. L. Blackstock, of the Blackstock Oil Company. When it was delivered to him in San Antonio, Texas, one day in 1937, it had been painted in a coat of insignia blue and cadmium cream Lockheed striping with gold edge. On June 10 of that year the Waco came to grief at Fort Worth. The remedy was to install four new wings, a new prop, new wheelpants, and cowling. In 1939 it began a round of exchanges. Late that year, the Waco was bought by E. K. Clevenger of Salem, Illinois, who sold it to Anthony Stinis, who flew his new possession to its new base, Floyd Bennett Field in New York, in June 1940. Stinis in turn sold the airplane to the Maine Air Transport Company, of Auburn, Maine, in 1941. Then came the war. The Waco joined a great many general-aviation aircraft being confiscated for domestic war work. It flew patrol missions for the Coast Guard in Nova Scotia, Maine, and Cuba.

The postwar years are not clearly documented, but the books show that the Waco traveled the United States from Seattle to Florida. In 1963 the airplane was purchased by Don Grimm of Des Moines, Iowa, from George Butcher of Battlefield, Missouri. Butcher had been keeping the aircraft in his barn, broken down for storage. In 1964 Hayes and his wife first saw the Waco—and instantly loved it.

Grimm kept the airplane active for several years and redid a good portion of the fabric. The metal still needed work. At the Antique Airplane Association fly-in at Blakesburg in 1971, the venerable Waco met its future. Wayne and Marie Hayes again spotted it and made up their minds.

But Grimm was not sympathetic. Repeated inquiries failed to move him, until personal reasons caused a change of mind. A friend on the antique-aircraft grapevine called Hayes with the news that Grimm might relent if a new offer were made. Relent he did—almost. The catch was that though the price was right, the season was wrong. The Waco's home base in Iowa had only a sod runway, which had been rendered unusable by the autumn rains. If there were a good freeze to harden it, the airplane could be delivered to a nearby hard-runway airport at Ames, Iowa, for Hayes to check it out.

Hayes transformed himself into an intense student of Midwestern weather. Marie remembers that many sleepless nights passed before the next day's weather report looked right to head for Ames. The big day was February 3, 1972. It was crystal clear and *cold*. Grimm was surprised to receive a phone call from Hayes—not from New Jersey but from Iowa. The reluctant seller had relented, and a deal was a deal, but you don't own and treasure an airplane for nearly a decade and then easily part with it. He didn't even try to disguise his sadness.

Indeed, the Waco has been easy to love. Hayes has never regretted giving up his staid Stinson Station Wagon for a plunge into the sometimes trying world of antiquing. The airplane flies with a surprising smoothness. It has handled many eight-hundred-foot strips with aplomb and climbs at a healthy twelve hundred feet per minute. Landing it short takes little effort, Hayes says. "You bring it in at about sixty over the fence, haul back, and it virtually flares itself." But the pilot must keep his attention on the landing surface. "It will do a perfect three-point on grass, but it's bad to drop the tail in first on a hard surface. I always wheel-land at a strange field, and the Waco is squirrely during taxi."

Taxiing is a challenge, because the Waco is equipped with a Johnson Bar, a contraption widely used before the advent of hydraulic aircraft brakes. This mechanical system of variable braking, which involves engaging and disengaging a long ratchet-stopped lever, makes the aircraft very demanding. Just the right amount of pressure must be put on each of the wheel brakes, which must then be released at just the right moment so the Waco will roll in the desired direction. Although hydraulic brakes came in in 1938, the Cabin Waco and its open-cockpit

Hayes at the controls of the Waco. Many aircraft designed in the thirties had panel layouts that were made to look as though they were in luxury cars, hence the oval on this example and on many others. Note also the tooled aluminum control column. Although today's T configuration in panel layout is undoubtedly more functional, it is the kind of craftsmanship and attention to form in this Waco cockpit that gives what would otherwise be a straightforward machine a distinctive character.

stablemate, the UPF-7, continued to be built with drum- instead of disc-type brakes.

Hayes's airplane cruises at 125 mph indicated, consuming 15 gallons per hour out of its two 35-gallon top wing tanks. Its slow-speed characteristics are excellent, due, in part, to its wing loading. Hayes reports that it has sensational rudder control, which is a great help in providing it with excellent straight-on behavior during stalls. Furthermore, spin recovery—the airplane is certified for spins—is easy, aided by a small cutout on the trailing edge of the lower wing at the root, which allows air to pass over the empennage in nose-high attitudes. In steep turns, very little back pressure is needed.

The Waco's drawbacks are those things that would cause most passengers to take one flight and make it their last. Like most airplanes that are more than a decade old, the Waco is hot and noisy, and trying to relieve one problem only aggravates the other. The cabin is so hot in summer that Hayes is forced to roll down the windows while in the air. Rolling down the windows increases the noise level. One can find it hard to tune out the rude roar of the airplane's seven-cylinder "Shaky Jake" 275-hp radial, as well as the accompanying chorus stemming from the high drag of wires, struts, fixed gear, and other items.

The Jacobs was installed by Hayes after it was assembled by Paul Gingrich, who worked for the Jacobs firm for thirty-seven years. Gingrich had bought up the remaining Jacobs inventory when the company closed down a few years ago. He has two warehouses full of parts to make into engines on special order for people like Hayes.

The Waco's engine, a model 755B2, has fifty hp more than the original and is fitted with an all-aluminum Curtiss-Reed prop, which is one of nine in this design built by the company. Unlike most modern aircraft engines, the Jacobs that powers this Waco has both a magneto and a distributor instead of dual ignition.

Although the airplane was conceived as a five-seater, Hayes limits his passenger load to three plus pilot. Out of the Waco's 3,480-pound gross weight, approximately 1,305 pounds make up the useful load. *Useful* is the word for the entire airplane—as is the term *well used*. It is active, it is healthy, and it is still beautiful. No wonder it seems to emit a happy chortle at idle.

OPPOSITE

The wings of the Cabin Wacos are among the most graceful and beautiful of any biplane ever built. This is best seen in flight, from a position forward and slightly above.

Spinach in flight over a Missouri field.

4

Spinach

You—John Innes—are sitting there, talking with the guys about how someone has tried to rip you off in New York. You're not even aware of the presence of your destiny lying like a heap of junk in the back of the hangar. So you go on telling these people at the Santa Paula Airport, California, how you really have wanted to restore an Eaglerock, after many years of absence from aviation. The fellows are sympathetic. Santa Paula is famous as a haven for antiquers.

That guy on Long Island was something else. You'd heard about his Eaglerock, with its 185-hp Hisso engine, waiting to be gobbled up. You flew to New York, and the owner asked that you send him a thousand dollars a month while he did the restoration. Just like that. He figured it would take two years. The flight home was painful at the least. That Eaglerock would have been a beautiful and unique restoration, just the sort of thing to break you out of the imprisonment of your promise made to the wife in 1945—to stay away from such foolishness. It is now 1966.

You wanted to share the misery, so you went to Santa Paula, and you told the story. You told the story—then what? Self-pity can go a long way, but it never takes flight.

Then someone says, "John, why don't you restore this?"

You turn to look at the gathering of debris on the floor. "What is it?" you ask.

"It's a 1936 Porterfield."

"I'd have to be out of my head to try to make an airplane out of that," you say. "It's a pile of junk!"

The cockpit of *Spinach*. Not quite adequate for IFR, but more than enough for hours of delightful flying. Innes has taken *Spinach*, or vice versa, back and forth across the United States on several occasions. The purpose of the elaborate warning system in the upper left hand corner of the cockpit is, according to Innes, "to scare the ducks."

No one says it, but you know: many beauties begin that way.

You remember, too, that you once flew a Porterfield, back in the thirties, when your head was full of airplanes, as now, and there was no holding you from the sky. Just on a hunch, you take down the N number to check it against your logbook. It's an impossible chance, of course, but it might be fun to see if . . .

The airplane is part of your destiny. Your logbook tells you that in 1943 you flew that very airplane—not just any Porterfield, but *that* piece of junk. Those stringers and pieces of fabric and those curiously shaped parts took you up and for twenty minutes supported you and protected you against gravity and the hard ground. The story begins to come back.

The airplane's name was *Spinach*. It was green, and that was what its first owner, actor Robert Cummings, named it. Forest green, really ugly, to Innes's taste. During World War II Innes was at Ogden, Utah, at a time when all private aircraft were being moved away from the coast of California. Even then, while the Japanese were assuming the defensive far across the Pacific, the security-obsessed authorities, having locked up all the Japanese-Americans in sight, were looking for things to worry about, so: get all those airplanes inland, pronto! That meant *Spinach*, too. One of Innes's friends stopped at Ogden while he was ferrying *Spinach* out of harm's way to Idaho. Innes flew the Porterfield for twenty minutes. He liked the machine. Okay. Just another flight, another scrupulously logged block of minutes . . .

Destiny stems from the past. Innes grew up in Colorado Springs, where Eaglerocks were manufactured. At age sixteen he embarked on building his own airplane. He carved the prop, he did everything, and he installed a Harley-Davidson motorcycle engine. That posed a problem, for he couldn't start the airplane by pulling the prop through in the normal way. So when he made the prop hub, he left the chain sprocket behind the prop. He could then wrap the chain around the sprocket and pull it by hand to start the engine.

But even so, this kid needed help, and he soon realized it. As he describes it, "I got the engine to start, all right, but every time it did, the

Innes's sense of humor can take curious forms, as in this "sale" sign in his hangar. The trombone helps express his love of Dixieland, which he plays in jams at the local pizza hut. He also takes the instrument with him on cross-country treks in *Spinach*, though how he fits it in that narrow fuselage with his other baggage is a mystery. He has entertained at many antique fly-ins and led the 1977 "Miss Blakesburg" parade.

Spinach in profile. The slight bulge in the belly is evident here.

end of the chain would whip around. I had chain marks on my little sixteen-year-old face, on my sixteen-year-old shoulders, and on lots of other places on my tender sixteen-year-old body." The project mercifully was dropped before any attempts were made to fly the plane.

At about that time, he was learning to fly in a homebuilt glider. He had been hanging around the Alexander Eaglerock factory, just keeping an eye out. He was a Boy Scout at the time, and as things turned out, his troop began the first aviation project ever sanctioned by the Boy Scouts of America. The troop made itself a glider, supervised by the Eaglerock department heads. The wood, fabric, metal, and other work had to pass muster by the pros. Then the boys learned to fly in it.

Those old days were good, no question about it. Visualize it. Colorado Springs, in a time when youth wasn't all that cynical. In the mid-1930s, a second world war seemed remote to teen-agers. You have this light, ungainly looking but flyable glider. And providing the tows is a Pierce-Arrow touring car, vintage 1917. The car had been a victim of a

Spinach's owner in profile. The slight bulge in . . .

governmental edict declaring these magnificent machines and other "old-fashioned" vehicles unsafe. So for three hundred dollars, this Pierce-Arrow went to a Boy Scout troop to be used for roaring down a runway with a captive glider in its wake. Innes remembers it well, describing it in a voice that trails off: "It was a great car. The headlights came up over the fenders, the gearshift and the brake lever were on the outside of the body . . ."

In 1943, Innes bought a Fairchild 22, his first real aircraft. "You could do anything in the world in that airplane, and I did," he says, again reminiscing about the high-wing, open-cockpit plane.

Then, in 1945, he took the pledge. It was like AA—but this was Aviators Anonymous. Stay off the throttle! But there are some habits you just can't kick. By 1966 he was hooked on a hangar wasteland called *Spinach*. For five hundred dollars he bought destiny.

In one of those strange arrangements that the twentieth century has made possible, John Innes works for his son, Rolly. His trade is graphics and design, which stood him in good stead in working on the Porterfield. For a while he had *Spinach* in disarray in the back of Rolly's trade-show display shop in Inglewood, California. Sometimes an airplane don't get no respect, and so it was one day with *Spinach*.

Innes's son, obviously regretfully, one day had to tell his father and employee, "Dad, get that junk out of here. You're taking up too much space." Well, an airplane *does* take up a lot of space, especially after it has been disassembled. So back the airplane went, to where Innes had first found it—Clay Graves's hangar at Santa Paula Airport.

Innes's graphic talent was badly needed for the restoration, for there were no plans to work from, just the old parts. He made drawings for the wings and built up his own rib jigs. Yet what do you do when the fuselage of the airplane is incomplete, bellyless, and there are no guides to work from? Innes designed a belly on his own, putting a slight

Innes holds one of the original wing ribs in its somewhat less than pristine state. Next to it is the jig he made to make up all the new ribs. In the background is *Spinach*, sans speed ring, in its hangar at Whitman Airpark in southern California.

bulge into it. Airplanes are among those few things in life that can go on looking just a little bit pregnant.

The ribs are unique in their construction. When the Porterfield was a new airplane, the ribs were secured to the gussets with brass or coated-steel nails. Each nail was held with a pair of tweezers and pounded in carefully so that its head just touched the surface of the gusset but did not penetrate the plywood. Innes saved a great deal of time by using a special staple gun with which he shot bronze staples into the gusset. In twenty minutes he could assemble a whole rib and make it stronger than the original.

Spinach is a beautiful, marvelously dated airplane to see and to fly—just watch the stall, she'll break suddenly, and the left wing drops like that—but the vibration level is memorable. That's the result of having no shock mounts, of bolting the engine directly onto the longerons. Four bolts hold it on. Originally the bolts were quarter-inch, but Innes had to ream out the mounts and put in larger ones. The engine is probably not the original one carried by this Porterfield, though who is to know? No logbook came with the airplane when Innes purchased it. Some Hollywood-happy type may have kept the documents because they were associated with Robert Cummings.

The present engine that *Spinach* bears—a LeBlond—was rebuilt by Ed Clark, of the Moth Aircraft Company in Hawthorne, California. During the rebuilding it was modified for greater power. Everything in the engine was replaced in the name of newness, so pistons, wristpins, and the master bearing were custom made.

But the LeBlond engine still poses problems in lubricating the upper valves. Innes is eloquent on the point: "There is nothing that is going to get much oil up there but an oilcan. You squirt it all around under the rocker arms. It flies all over the place when the engine is running." It can be very frustrating to watch an engine that used very little oil after rebuilding start to consume the stuff in prodigious quantities until it averages about a quart an hour. Innes's powerplant soon started consuming that much, seeping a lot of it out around the pushrods. (Innes later rebuilt and installed another LeBlond using a certain type of automotive piston ring that reduced oil consumption to next to nothing.) Innes decided one day to put an end to this problem by taking each of the tubes that cover the pushrods and dipping each end into the liquid insulation that is used to coat tool handles. It worked—too well.

A good example of paint and fabric work, showing how it is possible to make everything blend together—including protruding metal such as this aileron bellcrank.

Detail of the vertical stabilizer on *Spinach*. The top decal is one of only two allowed to be displayed in Los Angeles County. The Porterfield logo beneath the deputy sheriff's star was made up by Innes himself, copying the style of the aircraft's nameplate.

Everything was sealed too tight, so Innes had to chisel the solution off and live with the problem.

The cannibalism that can daunt some restoration projects was a frequent resort for Innes. The LeBlond's valves were machined from stainless-steel truck valves manufactured by General Motors. The shafts were turned down to the proper size and a small tulip-shaped crater was scooped out of the top of each valve.

The airplane's fabric is medium-weight Ceconite II. Up to the color coats, Innes covered it with nitrate dope. For the color, he used DuPont DuLux on the wings and Nason's Automotive Synthetic Enamel. To his mind, that type of paint holds its flexibility better than do others. He began with just a few coats of clear dope, then quickly switched to aluminum, because he felt that it fills in the pores of the Ceconite better. That way, when you sand, you sand on something besides the fabric.

One secret to practical antiquing is innovating on the inside and disguising it all with brilliant duplication on the outside. With those GM valves, for instance, one couldn't call this a genuine Porterfield, but does it matter when one can view the outward aspect and see what *has* to be a genuine 35-70 Porterfield resting all green and shiny on its three legs? The Porterfield Aircraft Corporation lettering on the horizontal stabilizer encourages the impression. It's a reproduction of the real thing that Innes made up using the silk-screen facilities available in his son's display shop. It was made exactly in the style of the original lettering, right down to the funny little short *e* stems. He used the design on the nameplate of the airplane as a guide.

But what's this, some savant might say, those three spearhead stripes on the sides of the airplane—they don't look authentic. They aren't. To Innes's eye, they were too fat as originally done, so he reduced their width by a quarter of an inch. He wanted them more delicate. And they are an improvement.

But if you can't take your eyes off the master stroke of decoration you might not even notice the stripes and other departures. In twenty-three-carat gold leaf, Innes has lettered the name *Spinach* with consummate care and grace. One can stare long and lovingly at it embellishing the green fuselage. *Spinach.* Thus is a whole family of vegetables ennobled—and an airplane, too.

But the oil, the damned oil. Seeping out, splattering back, at once necessary and wicked. The word *Spinach* withers in its petroleonic

Innes's rendering of *Spinach* on the side of the fuselage. He is a genius when it comes to this type of thing, to the extent of being able to do any kind of lettering. The result can be simple and straightforward or a complex combination of letters in various sizes, styles, and colors.

bath, and it must be cleaned regularly and delicately. Planning his strokes like a delicate painter, Innes regularly approaches his Porterfield's signature with a mild detergent solution. The gold leaf is very soft, the same kind that is used for lettering glass doors in offices. Gently, super gently, he follows the original strokes of the lettering, for otherwise the leaf will vanish.

The restoration took seven years to complete. In the end, Innes had created an airplane with a sweet-and-sour personality. Gentleness is one side of *Spinach,* but one must be prepared to be tough with the airplane. Like many tailwheelers of that era, the Porterfield seeks to weathercock during taxi, so one must handle it firmly. Yet, airborne, the Porterfield is stable and serene. Trimmed properly, it flies well hands off. The ailerons are stiff, but the response is good. Tap the stick and then relax the pressure—the plane will obey. Its cruise speed is 98 mph.

The wing is an M-6–type airfoil, as it is on the Taylorcraft. Landing must be done with full aft trim to prevent bouncing. The aircraft has a stabilizer trim, and holes in the rudder suggest that a previous owner had installed a small tab there, but Innes feels no need for it. After all, he says, "It's normal in this kind of airplane to have to apply rudder pressure for extended periods." One must also be very alert on the rollout, because the brakes are not particularly effective. *Spinach's* brakes represent one of the first attempts to introduce disc brakes to airplanes. Made by Goodyear, they consist of a copper-coated disc and a steel disc. Each disc has two little tabs, one on the outside, the other on the inside, fitting into a fluted slot in the hub. Innes suffered long with the brakes before someone said to him, "That's like the New Departure bicycle brake. You have to oil them." Innes oiled them, and they stopped their infernal squeaking, but that was all they stopped. Innes unoiled them immediately.

"The only thing the brakes are good for is as a place to plant your heel when somebody is propping you," he laments. "You can't even use them if you're trying to taxi, because you don't dare take your feet off the rudder pedals." It *does* have a steerable tailwheel.

The Porterfield has a curious history. It was the brainchild of Noel Hockaday, who wanted a homebuilt airplane project for a high school. Along the way, he induced financier Edward E. Porterfield, who had been president of the American Eagle Aircraft Corporation (not to be confused with the Alexander Eaglerock firm) until its demise in 1932, to fund the project. This led to the establishment of the Porterfield Aircraft Corporation in 1933. The first Porterfields were produced shortly thereafter, as a young boy named John Innes was getting up his enthusiasm for airplanes. Porterfields like the one Innes has were manufactured with various types of engines, including the Velie 55-hp, 70- and 90-hp LeBlonds, the 90-hp Warner Scarab, or other 40-, 50-, 65-, and 75-hp engines. The CP series Porterfields, which used the horizontally opposed Continental, Franklin, or Lycoming engines, were introduced in 1939.

The origins of this airplane were indeed varied and complex. In his own variations upon the Porterfield theme John Innes has been carrying on a tradition. But this point is often lost on the learned. At a fly-in, tongue cluckers will say to Innes, "It's a beautiful airplane, but it's just not original."

To which he will reply, "If I were designing the thing back then, it would be original, because that's the way I would have painted it."

In other words, I say it's *Spinach,* and to hell with it.

5

A Different Drum

This is a story of creativity, cannibalism—and contrariness. The contrariness applies to one Jim Younkin, a man of contrasts. The cannibalism applies to Younkin's Travel Air, a thing of beauty and venerable aspect. The creativity applies to both the man and the airplane.

Jim Younkin is professionally a man of the super-modern world, at home among transistors and thinking machines. His Piper Twin Comanche is a flying display case and test bed for electronic communications and navigational gear. Younkin has designed every autopilot in the current Edo-Aire Mitchell line. He's still with them, cooking up technological miracles. His career would make him seem like a totally steady individual with a single purpose—if it weren't for his need for contrast.

When he built model airplanes as a kid, in the 1930s and 1940s, the sort of equipment he has been designing as a man was merely speculative. He is one of a generation of young enthusiasts who, with brand-new degrees in electrical engineering and faith in the future of aviation, spread the seeds of progress among electronics firms during and after World War II. Younkin took a job at Collins Radio, because he would then be able to continue his education in electronics—he had the degree, but that was not enough—and still be in aviation. He stayed with Collins for a year, developing a sense of what kind of navigational

OPPOSITE
Jim Younkin's Travel Air 4000. These aircraft are easily identifiable in flight by oversize ailerons that protrude beyond the end of the wing tips. Only the top wings have ailerons, but the aircraft is still a credible aerobatic machine, though not at the air show level. (Waco's famous Taperwing model, one of which is still flown in air shows today by Bob Lyjak, was an exception in aerobatic ability.)

Jim Younkin at the workbench of his lab. Here he and his engineers turn ideas into working prototypes. A typical prototype will take two years to develop from the original concept.

equipment general aviation would need. But he came to the conclusion that, being employed in aviation, he was too close to it to see clearly the work that should be done. Sheer contrariness. Ask any career counselor.

He moved to Texas and got a job totally outside the aviation industry, so, as he puts it, "I could develop in my own backyard what I thought was a product that the industry needed." That product turned out to be a slaving system for directional gyros. He offered his device to Aviation Instruments, in Houston. They were delighted and wanted to buy it, but there was a hook to the deal. They also wanted to buy Younkin, so he could help to get the product started. Younkin can be contrary, but he can also be accommodating, so he accommodated his way back into the aviation business. In time, he joined Mitchell (later purchased by Edo and called Edo-Aire Mitchell Division) and was as totally immersed in aviation as he had been as a boy—at least before he discovered girls.

As his success at Edo-Aire grew, he found he had more leisure time and began looking for an avocation related to aviation. For a person like him, the answer was obvious: do a 180. If your direction professionally is toward ever-greater sophistication and modernity, do a 180-degree turn and head for the past.

He considered getting himself some plans for one of the many homebuilt airplanes that are popular these days. But he couldn't see flying such a creation to Oshkosh, Wisconsin, for the annual Experimental Aircraft Association fly-in, one of the major events of the general-aviation year, just to park it among dozens of others that would look exactly like it.

The alternative was an antique aircraft. It would be different, unique, and would take Younkin back to the days of wood and dope and the concentrated precision work that could make a young kid go cross-eyed as he built his models.

J. R. Younkin doesn't just buy an airplane and fly it and maintain it. That's just flying someone *else's* airplane, even though the papers say he owns it. In his eyes, the airplane is an extension only of the person who forms it. That's the foundation of the Younkin–Travel Air story.

The Travel Air he bought was part of a fleet of crop dusters that had been put on sale in Louisiana. This was in 1972, and the airplane had been dusting for at least twenty years before that. Travel Airs look light and lively, but they are also tough.

Younkin had had a special thing for Travel Airs since his childhood. For a while the Travel Air had been the snappiest plane going. Younkin's own Travel Air (serial number 798) was built in April 1929, the month of Younkin's birth.

He bought the machine in May and worked on it through July. He paused to go to Oshkosh for the annual jamboree and found himself again browsing about the homebuilts. A year of entropy set in. He started no homebuilt project, and the Travel Air waited unattended. Then came his next trip to Oshkosh.

In many ways, Oshkosh is like a great pollination. In from all over the country come unusual airplanes to gather for a week's worth of cross-fertilization. Homebuilts, antiques, classics, a highly polished collection of aeronautical flotsam and jetsam settles in, as at a rookery, and the pilots mill about looking, measuring, inquiring, and passing on information that often takes seed. Many an airplane that comes to nest at Oshkosh was hatched from ideas planted at a previous Oshkosh.

July 1973 was the time for Younkin's neglected Travel Air. An old Travel Air fuselage was on exhibit at the fly-in, opened up and accessible. Younkin homed in on it to take measurements and make sketches of such things as the seats, rudder pedals, and throttle quadrant. Back home, he built a rudder pedal—and a second rudder pedal, and a third, and a fourth. There was nowhere to go from there but for broke.

The individualist in him eschewed totally faithful restoration. This was to be *his* airplane, an antique he could fly, so he made it to suit himself.

That's where the cannibalism comes in. In Jim Younkin's Travel Air, other airplanes, or at least parts of them, are still flying. Yet the Travel Air's appearance is faithful to that of an original. Only a purist, an aeronautical pedant, would cavil over Younkin's achievement. Modification was part of this Travel Air's heritage, anyway. In the twenty years of its hard labor as an agricultural plane, it had been altered many times in many ways. The fuselage, for instance, was different in design from the original, except for the basic tubing. The landing gear was that of a Cessna 195. There were removable panels all the way down the side of the fuselage, except for where the hopper for the chemicals had been. Much needed to be done to restore the airplane. It was enough to make a modeling kid's heart sing.

The song had a few disharmonies. Younkin wanted that 195 landing gear off and a genuine Travel Air gear on. He scrounged and scrounged and finally had to settle on a genuine Travel Air left gear and an imitation right, with brakes and wheels taken from an old Fairchild PT-19. There's also some Stearman in the airplane: the top piece of the dishpan—the sheet-metal ring just aft of the engine—and the bottom part of the same piece.

The list of changes that Younkin had to make to bring the Travel Air up to his idea of an airplane is long. He started in July 1973 with a rudder pedal; it wasn't until May 1976 that he flew the airplane for the first time. It was backbreaking, and, some might say, pointless work. Pointless, perhaps, if you're willing to settle for just anything that flies. If you're that sort, you might not have done some of the things that make this Travel Air special.

You might have left the fuselage as it was, with 100 or so odd and extraneous fittings that had accrued over the years. Or you might have made a whole new fuselage from brand-new tubing in the time it took Younkin to remove the access doors, grind off the fittings, and bring the

The landing gear: Genuine (left), imitation (right), with brakes and wheels from a PT-19.

fuselage to the point where the control cables could be installed. Yours would have been a different and possibly inferior machine.

Much of Younkin's labor was meant to bring the fuselage into harmony with the 225-hp Lycoming R-680 engine. That Lycoming, by the way, is not the plane's original engine. Younkin brought harmony out of disharmony by creating new bulkheads and stringers throughout and by extensively modifying the forward portion of the fuselage. He took more pains with the compound curves than did the original manufacturer.

Watch antique-airplane mavens look at an antique airplane. What you see will tell you a lot about where their heads are. The expert approaches the airplane to register what it is and its general condition. If it's in ratty shape, he will pass on, like a gourmet offended by wine become vinegar. If the condition is respectable—if the paint is neat, the airplane clean, the metalwork or wood-and-fabric work tastefully done—he will zero in on the things that mark the restorer's signature. He begins with the cockpit.

The cockpit is where the pilot lives. It is really where the airplane lives. There rest its mind, its eyes, the limbs and intelligence that will take it into the air and prevent it from dying a crumpled mass on the ground. The cockpit is the signature both of the pilot and of the airplane, for if it is restored well, the cockpit does more than any other portion of the antique to bespeak its era, the *Zeitgeist* that provided its styling, its virtues, its flaws.

A cockpit can also be a reflection more of its individual creator than of a time. So it is with Younkin's Travel Air. The throttle quadrant is a duplicate of that of the Travel Air Younkin saw at Oshkosh and that inspired him to return to his own wasting plane. It is gracefully cut from aluminum. Every curve and edge is beautifully rounded and finished. The knobs were personally turned by Younkin in his machine shop. Lettering is hand-stamped into the metal.

The seats are reproductions of authentic Travel Air seats and have a sense of "old newness" about them as testimony to the fineness of their finish. The instrument panel is sparse in itself, but lush with history. Younkin photographed antique instruments and then had his instrument faces modeled after them. But Younkin of Edo-Aire stepped in to make sure that the insides of the instruments were up to date. The tachometer is a World War II electric model made to look like the old Joseph W. Jones tach, which dates back to World War I.

Cockpit of the Travel Air. The throttle is on the left side. Note the graceful curve on the rolled edge of the seat back. On the deck, inboard of each rudder pedal, are the heel brakes, one for each wheel on the landing gear. On the panel (left to right) are the magneto switch, the airspeed indicator, the tachometer in the center with the compass above it, the altimeter, the oil-pressure gauge, and the oil-temperature gauge. Very basic.

Younkin machined this throttle quadrant for his Travel Air in his own shop. Even though it is a new component, he gave it the same attention in design and execution that the original craftsman would have.

Younkin photographed, then silk-screened, the face of the "Jos. W. Jones" tachometer reproduced here (center). He also duplicated the compass (top) and Travel Air nameplate (bottom), with the serial number 798.

The easiest part of the airplane to rebuild was the wings. In fact, Younkin's Travel Air has advantages over the originals in strength and streamlining. The original Travel Air had quarter-inch steel tubing between the ribs on the trailing edge, and after being covered and flown for some time, the shrinking fabric would tend to pull the tubing inward between the ribs. To overcome that, Younkin used a V-shaped strip of aluminum for a stiffer trailing edge. The original Travel Air also had wire or tubing at the edges of the top wing. The edges don't take fabric covering well. Younkin made a smoother, more rounded edge out of wood.

The factory airplanes also had a half-inch gap between the center section and the upper wing on each side, and the gap was always irregular. The fabric would tend to pull the edge of the wing unevenly and distort the shape of the gap. Younkin installed plywood gussets—a sheet of plywood on either side of the gap—to keep the fabric from distorting the edges. His meticulous work resulted in a one-eighth-inch gap, which is very narrow for that airplane.

As a vestige of its ag-flying days, the Travel Air had squared-off wing tips, but Younkin wanted the original bowed-out shape. He cut off the tips and then re-extended them, adding new bows. The bows were larger than the originals, and Younkin's work made them stronger. Younkin made the ailerons from scratch. The airplane has ailerons on the top wings only.

The tail assembly also got the Younkin treatment, resulting in a smoother, more integrated appearance than that of the original, which had a wooden, two-piece horizontal stabilizer. After the fuselage was covered, the stabilizer could be plugged into each side. When the Travel Air had been used as an ag plane, the original stabilizer had been replaced with a one-piece metal one. Younkin opted for metal, too, adding sheet metal to the fuselage and replacing the now-rusted tailpost. The original strap-type hinge was put back in, replacing a pin-type one that was part of the ag-plane modification. This entailed putting a false trailing edge on the metal stabilizer by routing out a concave surface in a strip of wood to make the new trailing edge blend in with the horizontal stabilizer.

Younkin opted for wood, however, for the vertical stabilizer to recreate the airplane's original look.

Jim Younkin's Travel Air resides at Springdale Airport, near Fayetteville, Arkansas, a monument to patience.

As biplanes go, the Travel Air has a sharp, elegant look to it, but it is a strong performer. The ailerons are heavy, even sloppy, under certain conditions, but the airplane is docile in the stall and beautiful when spun—so says Younkin's son, Bobby, the aerobatic pilot in the family. The Travel Air cruises at about 110 mph and stalls around 55. Curiously, the airplane tends to wander in pitch. The elevator is so responsive that you can hardly read a chart as you fly. Trim it up, then take your hands off the stick, and the airplane will take on a life of its own.

So much for the bad news. The good news is that this bright red Travel Air is a kind of beacon, a spreader of happy tidings. Those cylinders almost nakedly pumping away causing a happy drone, the wires vibrating to the rushing wind, those wide wings, that virtually newly built fuselage, and Younkin's other refinements announce that independence, determination, imagination, flexibility, and the individual's strongest shot—contrariness—still flourish.

To Jim Younkin, the airplane is a living chronicle. "I look about the airplane and see days spent doing this and doing that," he says proudly. Not many men are fortunate enough to take the record of their days in their hands and lift it into the clouds.

Jim Younkin's Travel Air 4000 in a familiar environment—clear skies above sectioned flatlands. Need some navigation? Just pick a line—any line.

Susan Dacy's Stearman. The paint scheme, strictly her own, is unlike any other.

A Feminine Touch

6

Put the right kind of squint on it and it would be easy to see Susan Dacy as a symbol. That would be a mistake. The ingredients for "significance" are there, certainly. At seventeen, this girl had built her own Stearman, had done it herself, and had mastered the thing. Call what has driven her aggressive feminism, call it the youth revolution, call it the new individualism. It is easy to call it anything but what her achievement really meant—to her: her chance to fly when she wanted to. Another meaning can be put on it: tradition.

Susan Dacy sweated and strained in the back of a hangar at Dacy Airport in Harvard, Illinois, to have an airplane of her own. Stearmans are in her family. The Dacys, especially her father and brothers, Dave and Phil, restore them. Dave test-flies them. Before restoring her own, Susan sometimes had to beg for rides, and finally the anger got to her. In the tradition of many aviators who would not settle for being grounded, she obtained her airplane by recreating it.

Dacy Airport hosts one of the most active airplane dealerships in the Midwest. A lot of Cessnas are sold there. But the field, which has three grass runways, is also a hotbed of restoration fever. Something like a dozen hangars dot the airport, and in some of those structures are beauties of the past. Dave Dacy has a Stearman with a 300-hp Lycoming; Phil has a splendid Buecker Jungmeister; the president of the Stearman Restorers Association, Tom Lowe, bases his Stearman there; Loel Crawford keeps his highly photogenic Waco UPF-7 there; and among the many other Stearmans and other antiques one can also see a fine Ryan PT-22. In fact, Susan had considered restoring a PT-22, but she'd flown one and preferred the Stearman's lighter controls.

It helps when considering a Stearman to keep its own significance in mind. The Stearman model Susan chose was introduced in 1940 and became the Army Air Corps' PT-17 and the navy's N2S4. PT stands for primary trainer, and the Stearman was the doorway to flight for thousands of army, navy, and marine pilots. Whatever they flew later, they always remembered the Stearman, with its full-throated roar, its rough-tough exterior, and its reputation for ground looping. It is still a macho airplane in many pilots' eyes, so what was one very feminine fifteen-year-old lady named Susan Dacy doing putting one together in the back of a hangar in Harvard, Illinois?

Very simple. She wanted one of her own to fly. But as the work progressed, and as the frustrations began to work their will, it became more than that. She wanted no particular glory, but she also wanted no defeat. Her foes became fatigue and time and phenomena called crinkling and blushing, which had nothing to do with her skin.

Stearmans are hefty planes. Their careers didn't stop with the end of World War II. They were built so rugged—99 percent of the gear bolts on Susan's Stearman were installed in 1942—that they were commonly used as crop dusters in the sixties. When Susan addressed herself to getting those bolts out of the landing gear, she was taking on a taxing job. But Susan Dacy is an Aries, the sign of the optimist, which had to help. She got her first ride in a Stearman by prodding her brother into arranging one for her at a local air show. She was almost fifteen. The airplane won her over immediately. Only you don't just go out and get yourself a Stearman. There are plenty of unrestorable piles of junk lying around, but, as Dave Dacy puts it, "You look for a fuselage sitting on landing gear." He likes to tell of certain people who claim their restoration expertise: "Guys that say, 'We're perfectionists.' They're standard, coast to coast—and then their wings fall off."

Luckily for Susan, a 1942-vintage N2S4 rested in the back of a hangar at Dacy Airport. It had been there for five years, in pieces, a pile of good intentions on the part of an owner who just couldn't get around to doing the work. He decided to trade it for a Stearman the Dacys had just finished rebuilding. Susan had her chance—and her burden—before her.

She did the thing herself. She bought parts with money earned

Father helps daughter maneuver the Stearman out of the rain.

cleaning airplanes. Fortunately, the fuselage was in fair shape, and it came sandblasted. But there was much cleaning to do and all the control rods and instruments had to be installed. She rebuilt an entire wing. And she brought the engine to health, a struggle in itself.

This Stearman came with a 220-hp Continental engine. (Stearmans have been certificated for 220-hp Continentals, 225-hp Lycomings, 300-hp Lycomings, 450-hp Pratt & Whitneys, and a very few had Jacobs engines.) This one needed a good crankshaft, which was not easy to

The black wrinkle finish on these panels was the source of much frustration for Susan. The end result, however, is quite professional.

find, and Susan completely disassembled three run-out engines before she found a crankshaft that would do.

Rebuilding wings and performing similar major activities gives a dramatic flavor to antiquing, for the results of success are quickly and enormously apparent. The true agony often comes over little things that a spectator could quickly lose interest in, but things that one is judged for as much as for the condition of one's wing fabric or the set of the wheels. Getting a nice, even crinkle finish on the instrument panel was one of Susan's banes.

It isn't the doing, it's the redoing and redoing that get to you, the coming back yet one more time to get it right. She came back about twenty times. She would paint the panel and let it dry a bit before holding it in front of a heater to make the paint crinkle. The trick was to heat evenly, and that was tormentingly difficult. One side or another of the panel would come out fine, but not both. At last, they came out even.

And a sixteen-year-old antiquer, flushed with the blessings of Aries, could also impose frustrations on herself. She began wanting the classic Stearman look, the tires left exposed and the engine sticking out. Then, at an Antique Airplane Association fly-in in 1974, she saw one with wheelpants and a cowling. That was for her. However, one doesn't just put on a cowling. For a month, on and off, Susan (with some family assistance) labored over the welding and bracket installation to build the cowling's support ring. The same kind of hard, meticulous work went into the installation of the fiberglass wheelpants, which finally had to be discarded in favor of a stronger set.

With no previous experience, she did all the fabric work, using grade-A cotton to get the slick finish it can provide. Again, meticulousness, as also in getting the registration number, NI6SD, onto the tail. Lacking the proper stencils, she had to make them up, estimating the right size. It took three months of weekends to get a set that was acceptable. Again, frustration. It would look right while she was doing it, then the next day it would be all out of proportion.

Of course there were also unbidden spectators who wandered in to see what could be going on in the recesses of the hangar. Often vibes of skepticism, of condescension, emanated from them. They might as well have been wondering aloud when this girl was going to end her little joke.

The little joke also involved painting some fifty thin coats of dope on the exterior of the Stearman, with wet-sanding between every second or third coat. The result is a fine patina. Toward the end of the project, when it was time to paint, the Dacy family pitched in to help. The Stearman is basically green with white and gold trim. Suddenly things were speeding up. In July 1975, as the work seemed to be nearing completion, a series of very humid days brought on the problem of blushing (see page 181), in which the paint dries unevenly. Test after test without success began to eat into Susan's limited supply of enamel and dope. A paint company had made up a special batch to match a dime-store sample she had sent them. The matching had been difficult, and the company did not intend to make a second batch.

Finally, at 2:00 A.M. on a Friday morning, the humidity dropped, and the Dacys set to work. On Saturday, Susan applied the gold trim. On Sunday, the wings were put on.

Confounding the skeptics: with the results of her handiwork in the background, Susan Dacy tells admirers what it took to restore her big biplane.

The following Wednesday, twenty-two months almost to the day from the beginning, Dave Dacy climbed aboard Stearman NI6SD and steered it to the grass runway.

To Dave, the Stearman flies lighter than a Waco UPF-7, a Travel Air, and even a Bellanca Citabria. Its control balancing is smoother than that of other antiques, and it behaves well when put to the test. Its power-off stall speed is fifty-six knots, and when it stalls, the nose falls through cleanly, straight ahead, after the airplane has given fair warning with ailerons and shuddering stick that the stall is impending. The Stearman loops well and is smooth in an eight-point roll. It takes a bit of time for spin recovery, but there isn't a maneuver it is incapable of.

Dave Dacy has tested every Stearman the Dacys have restored. He takes the plane to 3,000 feet above the airport—just in case he has to glide back down. His main concern is for the engine, for there is little chance that anything else is going to come apart. The key is oil pressure. If the oil pressure is lost, he keeps the engine going. Shutting down an engine right away can be a sign of panic. He heads for the runway, and only when he knows he's got the field made does he shut the powerplant down. No point in ruining an airplane just to save an engine.

His sister watched as he took her Stearman through its first paces. To her, it seemed a touch unreal that after all those months it was up there, flying. She had started the project before she had even soloed. Now she had her private license—her checkride had been in a Stearman.

The inevitable bug about the airplane was the brakes, a typical problem with Stearmans. The airplane is unusual in having chrome-plated drums. They last a long time, but they will sometimes glaze the brake shoes. A deglazing at an auto shop is the cure.

The closest thing to a triumphal march Susan Dacy would enjoy after her success was a formation flight of the Dacy airplanes, including her Stearman, to the 1975 AAA Fly-in at Blakesburg, Iowa. At the fly-in, however, she was treated strangely by some of the men who had themselves won prizes for the quality of their Stearman restorations. Later, she would sit back and laugh at the mix of reactions, from young males putting on the heavy moves to the most common response, admiration. There were the carping criticisms, too, for little things remained to be done. Susan accepted it all with poise and good humor, at home with her achievement. She pointed out that the plane had just been completed, so what did they expect? Or she would say, "Oh, gee, how thoughtless of me. Want to go for a ride?" which did the trick. As always, there was the standard line about a woman's place being in the kitchen. "If they'd seen me in the kitchen, they would think differently," she says.

She is getting her education at Southern Illinois University in Carbondale to prepare her for an aeronautical career. She will also fly her Stearman, and other planes, to build time toward her acceptance as a professional pilot. A major part of her bachelor of science degree will be her work toward an Airframe & Powerplant license, which would make her a certificated mechanic. The university has accepted her work on the Stearman as a substitute for an eight-week practical-experience course for A & P candidates. Her Stearman is hangared near the school, and she is doing what she did in high school—using study periods for day-to-day practice in the air and coordinating the days she gets "sick" with the dates of antique fly-ins.

She is, in fact, a compulsive flyer. She has flown various Cessna singles, a Cub, and a Champ, which provided a winter's frigid flying. It can get terribly cold in Illinois during the winter, and any pilot who resists the temptation to let flying go for an icy day and stay home has

Brother Dave's Stearman, powered by a 300-hp Lycoming. Dave has given many exceptionally smooth aerobatic performances in this machine. He is equally proficient aerobatically in his brother's Buecker Jungmeister.

got to be strange or special. In January 1975, Susan Dacy endured the knives of winter in the Champ for twenty-five hours of flying time, not to mention what were perhaps even more hellish hours of preflighting. That, too, is part of aviation tradition—the simple determination to fly, come frostbite or high fever.

Susan Dacy is not a self-glorifier, but she is a self-tester, as the existence of her Stearman itself proves. She has tried to teach herself aerobatics in her airplane, but she realizes that she needs instruction. Teaching oneself aerobatics is like teaching oneself high diving, pole vaulting, or ballet dancing: it is hard to be graceful and easy to fall. Trying a loop, one can find oneself stalling out of it and seeming to fall out of the sky. An errant roll can leave one wondering which side is supposed to be up.

Susan has denied her detractors, who refuse to admit her accomplishment, the satisfaction of seeing her fall prey to a ground loop in a Stearman. As has been said, the Stearman has a reputation for whirling about itself on landing, though there is open debate as to how true that is. Dave Dacy will tell you, however, that if you do ground-loop or let the plane swerve (it usually goes to the left), you are in for expensive repairs. "You get the wing tip, especially the bottom wing, and the aileron, and you've got more problems than you think." Spars break—it doesn't take too much, not even a ground loop. Added to these dangers is the fact that because Susan Dacy is a young woman—young girl, to the insurance people—her insurance is eight hundred to nine hundred dollars a year, which is high. Still, she has never had any sort of accident.

At fly-ins and at Dacy Airport, she is often watched like a hawk. Coming in over the fence at her home field she lets her Stearman find the turf gently and she keeps it rolling straight and true, thinking of those waiting for an "incident" that doesn't happen, thinking, "Gee, I hate to disappoint you all."

That's the gritty side of her story, and it's perhaps inevitable until old ideas about women are completely laid to rest. The better and more real side of her story lies in her acceptance by antiquers who know good work, hard trying, and success when they see it. It started with her brothers, who came more and more to accept her as a kindred spirit as she labored in the back of that hangar. And it has spread among her fellow antique craftsmen, who ultimately will let prejudice yield to their appreciation for a good old airplane.

John Bowden and his son Terry head up the hill on the Bowden family farm to where the Robin is hangared.

7

Keeping the Faith

His most trusted mechanic advised him not to undertake the restoration, but John Bowden would not be swayed. There was a boyhood memory of a Curtiss Robin, its fuselage draped over a tree branch while a junk dealer cut away its engine with a torch to sell for scrap. That image was too strong, like the recollection of a pragmatic father who wouldn't let the sixteen-year-old Bowden save the plane from destruction.

So when, in 1968, a particular Robin kept appearing among the advertisements in *Trade-A-Plane*, the foremost trading journal in general aviation, Bowden decided to buy it. With an aircraft mechanic friend, he flew up to Seymour, Missouri, to take delivery. Upon seeing the Robin, a skeptic would probably have turned around and gone home, for time had taken its toll on N82H. There wasn't much to suggest that it might be airworthy. But then anyone who becomes an antique owner by definition cannot be a skeptic. "She'll fly to doomsday," claimed the seller confidently, "if you don't crowd her."

It took four people nearly three hours to start the Robin—one in the cockpit, two outside on the crank of the inertia starter, and a small boy with a fire extinguisher on the sidelines. Fortunately, the return flight to Texas was uneventful. The 560 miles were flown in 7 hours and 45 minutes, with two fueling stops and nothing worse than the loss of an exhaust stack somewhere over Oklahoma.

Insurance contract writers talk about "acts of God," and it was evidently such an act that destroyed the records of the N82H's earliest years. It flew first on July 6, 1928, was mounted on Edo 3300 floats, and suffered the loss of its original logbooks in the Hartford, Connecticut, flood of March 1936. The right wing was extensively damaged and many of the ribs had to be replaced.

Then followed a succession of owners, periods of storage, and periods of activity. The Robin was variously re-covered, doped, and painted; overhauls were performed on the Curtiss Challenger engine; in 1938 the tail skid was replaced by a wheel. By all accounts, 1940 was an especially busy year. In the hands of J. E. Grant, of Baltimore, N82H flew all over the East Coast. After World War II the cycle of inaction, relicensing, and serviceability carried on until, at last, the Robin alighted at John Bowden's farmside strip near Lampasas, amid the rolling grasslands of central Texas.

Bowden's Robin taxis out to the "runway" on the family farm.

Nobody wanted to take on the job of restoring it. Shop after shop in the area refused the work. Finally S. K. Holmes, the FBO* and head mechanic for the Taylor, Texas, Airport, who had serviced Bowden's airplanes for years, was persuaded to change his mind. Holmes had gained his A & P license back in 1932 and had cultivated a special interest in the wood-and-fabric workmanship of the twenties and thirties. He himself used to barnstorm with a Challenger-engined Robin. So he was able to bring not only immense experience but also intuition to the task at hand.

That task was daunting, as Holmes had warned it would be. It began in the summer of 1971 and took nearly four years. The entire airframe was stripped and carefully gone over for signs of distress. Questionable sections of steel tubing, like portions of the longerons that had rusted out, were replaced. Then the frame was sandblasted and repainted. Inspection revealed that the horizontal stabilizers would have to be rebuilt, which meant straightening the ribs and replacing the spars and leading edges. One of the springs in the landing gear oleo struts was found to be completely broken up. It proved impossible to find an identical one, so in the end, Holmes took the springs from a PT-19 gear he had lying around and shortened them to fit. There was a lot of uncertainty about this, for the replacements were not as stiff as the originals, so Bowden and Holmes feared the whole thing might bottom out once the airplane was reassembled. In any event, the modified gear has turned out to be a great improvement. It is neither too soft nor too hard, even on the cow-pasture runway that Bowden uses every time he flies the Robin off its hilltop home.

Practically every piece of wood in the airplane was renewed, with one exception—the plywood stiffeners bolted to the wing ribs. The Robin was the first production aircraft with stamped aluminum ribs. However, these ribs proved not quite strong enough, and the government accordingly issued an Airworthiness Directive that each rib should be reinforced with an eight-inch plywood slab on one side. Throughout the restoration every attempt was made to use existing wood components as patterns, for some of the parts were so worn that it was impossible to determine their original shape.

*Fixed Base Operator. At most airports an FBO may buy and sell used and new aircraft, give flight instruction or run a flight school, rent aircraft by the hour, and may be involved in repairs or rebuilding as well as air taxi services, chartering, aerial photography, and selling fuel and supplies.

One setback occurred when a helper in the shop, having carefully removed the pieces of the wood door frames, neglected to code them. The result was a small pile of sticks that were good for kindling but not much else. Eventually, Holmes designed a new framework for the doors. The simple steel tubing of the Robin's fuselage outlines the apertures but not the doors themselves, so a little imagination was called for.

Lady Luck played her part in the renewal of the engine cowling. This comprises more than a dozen separate pieces and originally was one of the Robin's selling points, because it allows easy access for maintenance. There was no great difficulty in reproducing the various panels, however; the rear ones had a set of holes about two to four inches across, each with its edge rolled inward around a wire rod. This technique, called hemming, reinforces the edge and leaves a smooth surface. Bowden wanted to hem the cutouts of his duplicate panels, but he was at a loss to find the proper machine. None of the metalworking shops in the area had one.

Then, by chance, Bowden mentioned his predicament to an old friend, Ira Mashburn, who had been a tinner before he retired. A tinner specializes in making water tanks, gutters, buckets, and such out of metal. "I've got a hemming machine," said Ira. "It's buried under a load of junk at the bottom of a corn crib on the farm. Come over and borrow it anytime." Bowden was able to dig the machine out and spent one whole winter working the pieces of the cowling, using up two eight-by-four sheets of aluminum in the process. Cutting and hemming, as it turned out, was the "easy" part; it proved harder to get the Dzus fasteners properly aligned with their mountings.

The toughest job of all was rebuilding the 185-hp Curtiss Challenger engine—probably the first double-row radial, incidentally, to be fitted to a production airplane. At San Antonio, where the stripped engine components were taken for analysis, it was determined that the pistons and cylinders would have to be reworked. The San Antonio shop turned the cylinders 0–020 oversize, while the pistons were sent

OPPOSITE
The gear on Bowden's Robin has been modified slightly by the replacement of the original springs with those from a PT-19, which were shortened to fit the Robin's struts. Although there was some doubt whether the new springs would be satisfactory, since they were not quite as stiff as the originals, in fact they turned out to be superior.

to Jahns's* in southern California with a request that they make new ones.

They turned out a beautiful set of pistons, better and stronger than the originals, with lots of webbing inside. But these were also heavier, and the FAA wouldn't buy the difference. It said that the additional weight would result in an unacceptable increase in bearing loads. Bowden was faced with a choice: either fit the heavier pistons and license the Robin in the Experimental category, or lighten them up to original specs for compliance with the Standard category. After so much effort to achieve the latter classification, the restorers felt there could be no compromise at this point. They solved the problem by milling off some of the metal inside the pistons and then weighing and further milling all six until they matched.

The difficulty in the restoration process that caught them most by surprise was encountered as the engine was being reassembled. Explains Holmes: "After all the engine parts were ready, we began to put it back together. Everything was going along smoothly. We installed the pistons, pins, and so forth on the master rods—the engine turned nice and free. Then we put the pistons and cylinders on the link rods. Lo and behold, the crankshaft wouldn't turn. We looked in and saw that the balance weights on the crankshafts wouldn't clear the piston skirts."

*Jahns's is probably the best-known custom fabricator of pistons for hot rods, dragsters, etc.

Bowden points out a cutout in the engine cowling of his Curtiss Robin where the wire backing has worn through the rolled edge of the cowling metal, necessitating a new "hemming" job.

S. K. Holmes (left), who did most of the restoration work on the Robin, and John Bowden.

There was a big silence at that particular moment. Bowden knew they had undercut the new pistons to match the originals, so it was decided to take the whole thing apart again and do some measuring.

When Bowden and Holmes compared the master rods with the link rods, they found that there was a difference in length between the two. They figured that the rods had been designed that way, because if the link rods had been the same length as the master rods, they would not have cleared the bottom of the cylinder—so instead of cutting off the cylinder, the designers shortened the link rods.

Bowden and Holmes compared the measurements of the original pistons with those of the new set. They found that they had to take 0–040 off the piston skirts to make them clear the balance weights. The pistons were reweighed, and after a little more machining to match them up, they were installed in the engine. Everything then worked fine.

"It's interesting to note that the Challenger can never have a smooth, even-running sound because of this difference in the master- and link-rod lengths," says Bowden.

Information for the timing of the engine was discovered in a rather unusual place: a crankshaft counterweight. About forty words had been

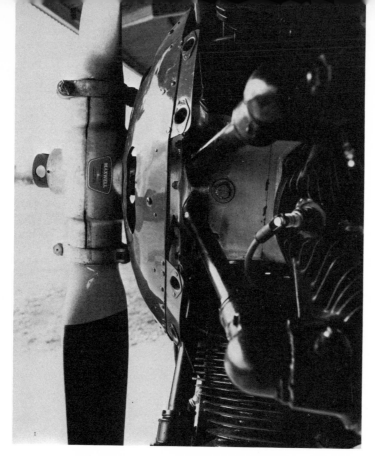

Removing the plug between these two pushrod tubes allows one to read information etched onto the crankshaft counterweight that describes how to time this Curtiss Challenger engine.

The Robin takes off, using only a fraction of the runway. Its excellent short-field performance is due in no small part to its thick, wide, high-lift wing.

etched into the weight and may still be seen even when the engine is fully assembled, after a certain plug, resembling a drain plug, is removed from the crankcase shell.

Throughout the rebuilding of the Curtiss Challenger, Bowden made an intensive search for an original manual. After many months of searching, he discovered a fellow antiquer who had one and copied all the specs from it for the aircraft's permanent records, so that any future rebuilder will have this at his fingertips.

The Robin is "a little stiff" to fly, says Bowden. He attributes this mainly to the control linkages, part of which are pushrods held in place by bronze bushings that are lubricated with a wad of grease on the finger. Nevertheless, the high-lift wing makes this a real STOL machine. At the local airstrip in Bowden's hometown of Lampasas, the first turnoff (really the run-up area) is about two hundred feet from the end of the asphalt; landing into an eight-to-ten-knot headwind, he can usually make that first turnoff. With only one person aboard, a little back pressure and a surge of power is needed to get the tail down.

Under favorable conditions, the Robin will indicate a steady 90

The Robin chugs along at a ninety-mph cruise, its slow-turning engine indicating 1,350 rpm.

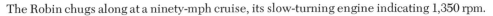

mph at 1,350 rpm. In this cruise régime, the Challenger engine consumes 8.5 gallons per hour. There's a fail-safe intercom for communication between the pilot and his two passengers in the back: a spiral notebook. Cabin noise is the bane of all old aircraft, and the Robin is no exception. Still, such discomfort hasn't kept Bowden, his wife, Glenna, and their son Terry from making long journeys to antique aircraft gatherings.

The Robin has been selected as the "chapter choice" at fly-ins organized by regional branches of both the Antique Airplane Association and the Experimental Aircraft Association. It was picked as Grand Champion at the Houston Sport Aviation and Classic Show in May 1975, and at the North Texas Regional Air Meet in June of that year. The most significant award of all was the Sweepstakes Trophy, presented at the August 1975 Invitational Fly-in of the AAA at Blakesburg, Iowa—without a doubt the biggest event in the antiquer's calendar, attracting the most outstanding restorations in the United States. The Robin won out of more than 350 competitors.

John Bowden doesn't care too much to fly the airplane locally. "It's just a curiosity to most folks, and people not familiar with antique aircraft can't possibly appreciate the work that went into restoring it. I would much rather go to the trouble of taking the Robin several hundred miles to a gathering of fellow enthusiasts."

When you actually see the ancient machine take to the sky, or sit in it as it plows its way forward a few hundred feet above Texas hill country, chugging along, or watch the struts vibrate like crazy, there isn't a single thing that reminds you of today.

You find your thoughts drifting a little, to another era in aviation, when, without benefit of sophisticated formulas, a little fabric and a few pounds of metal were fashioned by a handful of men into a practical touring airplane.

8

American Dream

Think about the American dream. What is it? Is it, perhaps, to have something to work at that you love and that keeps you going? To have something unique, beautiful, and pleasurable beyond what the tax collector may exact or time may confiscate? Something that can carry you and your family beyond the usual daily life? That something is not a bad definition, and it is not unachievable. It calls for imagination, daring, and love, for hard work and strength. But it is achievable.

Charles LeMaster has done it. Drive by his house someday, and if you don't gasp with wonder or sigh with love, forget nostalgia or antiquing, for there you will see an immaculate realization of the American dream—a working, breathing, eminently satisfying Ford Trimotor.

It would be easy to pooh-pooh the idea. Anyone who tries to run a Trimotor on a regular basis has an idiot for an accountant, and his accountant has a cretin for a client. Yet consider that the only reason this Trimotor isn't in a hangar is that it's so profitably active that it doesn't pay, in money or human energy, to keep trundling it into shelter. So out it stays, weathering the elements, ready every hour to justify itself.

Just by existing as it does, almost perfectly restored, the Trimotor justifies itself as its breed has done since the first Trimotor went into

OPPOSITE
The LeMaster Ford gets the go-ahead from a flagman during the EAA convention at Oshkosh, Wisconsin. Note the control cables on the exterior of the fuselage. The hatch above the copilot can be opened for climbing out and checking the fuel tanks.

service in a small airline operation between Detroit and Cleveland, in 1926. Only 199 Trimotors were built, between 1925 and 1932, but they became an institution, as crucial to the growth of aviation as another Ford product, the Model T, was to the growth of the automobile.

In 1925, Henry Ford bought the Stout Metal Airplane Company, which had produced, the year before, an eight-passenger transport. The Stout Air Pullman was made entirely of metal and had a corrugated skin, something unusual for the time, except for the Junkers F13. It even had a tubular aluminum framework, actually an aluminum alloy called Duralumin. Ford's interest in the Air Pullman stemmed from his desire to match what the Germans had accomplished in creating the Fokker Trimotor, which had established an excellent record for reliability in the Ford Reliability Tour, a nineteen-hundred-mile endurance test that Ford thought would serve to prove the usefulness of the airplane to the general public.

The Fokker had been developed from a single-engine airplane that was similar to the Air Pullman. Simple practicality—a Ford passion—dictated that to match such performance, an American should find a similar single design and develop a multiengine airplane from it. The Ford Trimotor was the result.

It should be remembered that in 1926 Lindbergh had not yet flown the Atlantic. Aviation was still regarded as a hazardous occupation appropriate only for the military and hell-bent-for-death daredevils. Yet the Trimotor soon began to create a sense of confidence in aviation. So much so that in 1932, its last year of production, presidential candidate Franklin Delano Roosevelt used one to campaign in. The Trimotor also became part of an ingenious scheme to span the continent faster than mere trains could do, by flying people by day and letting trains waft them along at night.

Such is the hunk of tradition that sits beside the home of Charles and Dianne LeMaster. Its history is part of the enormous appeal this airplane has for people all over the country. Today an airliner is an airborne motel, complete with movies, bar, restaurant, and virtually no sensation of flight. It may take you 35,000 feet into the air, but you might as well be 35 feet off the ground in your house.

That's not how it was when the Trimotor carried fifteen passengers instead of the hundreds that may crowd a 747 today. Then there was the noise of three large radial engines and the buffeting that can come with

An airliner cabin, circa 1929. Every passenger in the Ford has a terrific view, making the aircraft ideal for sightseeing rides. In addition, there is plenty of headroom for an aircraft of this size, and there is no spar on the cabin floor to stumble over.

low-level flying. And a sense of daring. *Nothing* was automated then. The pilots earned their pay every mile of the way, and the passengers participated simply by having put their faith into the embracing arms of the aviation dream.

There are people who remember those days and would like to recapture them, and there are people who have read about them and are eager to cut for themselves even the thinnest slice of history by actually riding in a Ford Trimotor, if only for a precious few minutes. That is what Charles LeMaster trades upon.

He had once been part owner of a Trimotor for spraying crops. Spraying can be profitable, but along with its hazards can come boredom. And it did have its unpleasant moments. As he recalls it, "There was always some biddy calling and saying, 'You didn't kill this,' or 'You killed my garden.' And then the EPA [Environmental Protection Agency] came in." (Ironically, the EPA operates its own small fleet of air- and water-pollution research aircraft, at least one of which—an extensively reworked B-26—can lay claim to antique status. Another, a Beech 18, or Twin Beech, has been modified to have tricycle gear and two turboprops. These fastidiously maintained aircraft are *not* used for VIP transportation.)

LeMaster noticed that his airplane drew attention. That highwinged, strangely graceful yet strangely awkward beast (a Trimotor can be both at the same time) brought people looking as it ranged over the crops. At airports, it even attracted TV cameras. So, in the summer of 1973, he tried an experiment.

He installed a few seats in the Trimotor and went barnstorming. That, in itself, was a return to earlier times. Like the old barnstormers, the LeMasters went for the profits and the fun of aerial joyriding and found both. So much so that in 1976, after twenty-three years in the spraying business, LeMaster gave up vegetable buzzing. Barnstorming pulled in more cash than spraying.

Actually, he took a detour. He had had only an interest in the Trimotor, and that he quickly sold. He wanted a pioneer transport of his own, and he found it in a Boeing 247, the only one then flying. It was an ironic decision, for the 247, with its retractable gear and streamlined body, was the evolutionary link that ended the era of boxlike transports like the Trimotor. And there was a further irony. The very modernity of the 247 made it less attractive to the 1970s public than the Trimotor. No matter that it was one of the last of its tribe, the 247 was too modern. So

The Ford takes another load of passengers back in time fifty years. Large, loud, but not lumbering, the Trimotor once represented a height of transportation luxury.

LeMaster turned back to the twenties' look of the Trimotor. But where to find one?

South America is a good repository of Trimotors, so LeMaster began his inquiries there and also advertised in various domestic publications. No dice. He then fell back on another plan, making up a list of every Trimotor known to be in the United States and phoning every known owner. The barrier seemed insuperable. No owner would even put a price on his Trimotor.

There was one last hope. American Airlines had been using two Fords for publicity and had run out the string of PR benefits. One of the old airplanes was slated for the Smithsonian—it now resides at the new National Air and Space Museum in Washington—but what about the second? LeMaster called American, only to learn that the Trimotor had been sold—but on the basis of a verbal commitment only . . .

As LeMasters relates it, "They said they would be glad to let me see it and that it was in Tulsa. I was on a charter trip to Denver at the time. I didn't bother going home first—I went straight to Tulsa."

And there it was. Squatting on front main wheels and tailwheel, with two engines slung under the wings and another protruding from the proboscis. He told the executives from American that he wanted this airplane, not as a museum piece but to fly, and that seemed to impress his audience. The slated buyer, in fact, had been planning to put the airplane in a museum, but to LeMaster's relief, he was proving hard to find to close the deal.

Two months went by. The slated buyer went on this trip and that, out of reach, while the airplane waited. The deal remained open, and LeMaster steamed. Finally he could stand it no longer. He called American and was told, "We'll call you back in fifteen minutes." LeMaster's heart stopped. Had he barged in on the consummation of the deal? Had he called just in time to hear the worst? He waited the full fifteen minutes and a bit more.

The phone rang.

"Chuck, if you want that airplane, it's yours."

Breathlessly, LeMaster said, "I'll be there in the morning." The next day he was in Tulsa, writing the check.

LeMaster's Trimotor was already a veteran of show business. It had been part of American's static display at the New York World's Fair in 1964–65. From stardom it had gone to mothballs and was in storage when LeMaster grabbed it.

It quickly became the old story for an antiquer. First, you sweat to find or get the airplane, and then you start all over—making the airplane you've bought. The making of this Trimotor took 287 days. As many as six people worked on the Ford at one time, which was a sizable crew; but the key to the project was a single genius, a man who could make the engines sing.

Henry Thompson does with radial engines what great organ builders do with their complex musical machines. Conveniently, he was in Tulsa when the restoration took place, working for Miller Aircraft Engines. He has since deservedly gone into business on his own. His task was to make the three 450-hp Pratt & Whitney Wasp Junior engines of LeMaster's 1929 vintage 5-AT-C Trimotor sound like new. (The 5-AT series of Fords, by the way, had been developed under the encouragement of Charles A. Lindbergh, in 1928. Lindbergh wanted the Trimotor to be able to compete against the Fokker F-10 transports, which were also equipped with Wasp engines.) Thompson worked his magic to the point where LeMaster was able to fly the Trimotor from Ottumwa, Iowa, to Los Angeles and then to Ottawa, Kansas, using only two gallons of oil for the whole trip. That is extraordinarily efficient, and the engines still run that way.

The structural work involved some necessary modifications. The original Trimotor came with Johnson Bar brakes, a common feature of flying antiques. The Johnson Bar is a ratchet affair that must be alternately set and released according to the amount of braking needed. The pilots of Island Airlines, based in Clinton, Ohio, who until recently flew a Trimotor on a regularly scheduled basis, have kept their Johnson Bar and present an interesting bobbing and weaving display as they work the brakes on taxi. LeMaster decided to go with more modern toe brakes. He also decided to replace the original oleos with a system from a Republic P-47 fighter and the wheels with those from a Lockheed Lodestar. Thus, near-antiques service a classic.

As the airplane was worked over, LeMaster could appreciate its fine construction. The corrugated skin—virtually its hallmark—is of Duralumin, the aluminum alloy, and is held together with rivets and

The three Wasps of the Trimotor.

gussets. The wing is made from a heat-treated aluminum alloy, which was first riveted together, then covered with corrugated Duralumin. There are no exposed rivets in the surface of the wing, the span of which is 77 feet, 10 inches, with an area of 835 square feet. The wing is so thick that each side is able to feature a crank-down cargo compartment for a 400-pound load.

On June 12, 1973, after $100,000 worth of restoration, Charles LeMaster's restored Ford Trimotor was flight-tested, and a way of life for the LeMaster family began.

To taxi the Trimotor you must make S-turns, weaving back and forth along the taxiway to compensate for the airplane's limited visibility in a three-point attitude. To turn when on the ground, you must apply a good deal of brake, for the Trimotor's tailwheel is steered with shock cords, even though the rudder is attached directly to the pedals. On takeoff, the tail comes up smartly and quickly, and the visibility problem disappears. Veteran pilot Max Conrad, who has flown LeMaster's airplane extensively, verifies that the takeoff roll is less than 1,000 feet at maximum gross weight, which is 12,500 pounds, under LeMaster's STC. Rotation is at 75 mph, and the climbout is approximately 950 feet per minute on a standard day. The airplane's payload is 4,331 pounds.

Trimmed for cruising, the Ford will do about 110 mph true airspeed. The three engines burn approximately 65 gph for about 5 hours of flying, with an hour's reserve. The fuel rests in one 126-gallon tank in each wing and in a 103-gallon tank in the center section between the wings.

With a glide ratio of 8.7 to 1, the Trimotor, say both LeMaster and Conrad, "flies like a big Cub." It lands at about 65 mph and one must guide it carefully onto the ground, for it is eager to float. The rollout is roughly 1,000 feet in a three-point attitude and 1,500 feet when wheeled on.

Such a plane is, of course, more than performance. When ready for its new life, it bore its original markings, registration number, a United States flag, and its Pratt & Whitney engine number. It also sported a name, *The Kansas Clipper*, on the nose.

The cockpit of the airplane is a combination of the simple, both ancient and modern. The panel has three rpm gauges, a clock, a vertical speed indicator, engine instruments, manifold pressure gauge, artificial

On the Ford's tailwheel, the shock cords are visible at the level of the axle.

The cockpit has been reworked somewhat. The radios on the floor are all modern King units. On the ground, a seat belt attaches the two control yokes to keep the controls from flapping around in the wind.

The Ford cockpit looking aft. The flight deck floor is slightly higher than that of the cabin. Note the eight-track tape player (since removed by Scenic Airlines; see note, page 110) near the ceiling, probably not a factory-installed option.

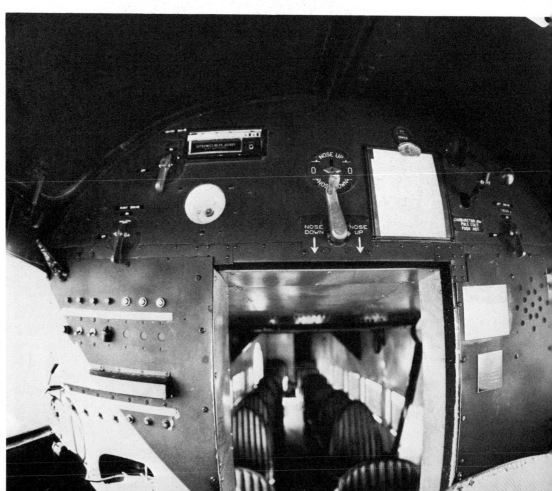

horizon, directional gyro, compass, altimeter, omni head, outside temperature gauge, and a cylinder temperature gauge. Below are the radios and transponder. Behind the pilot are the carburetor heat switch, nose trim, and a few other knobs. The pilot and copilot sit on the original seats, as do six of the fifteen passengers. The dual yokes have the braided leather reminiscent of a time of fine workmanship. The yokes call for work, though, for the controls of the airplane, which has a low wing loading, are heavy. The rudder and elevator cables are strung outside the airplane.

Passengers enter through a door at the tail and walk uphill to their seats, which are made of upholstered leather with corrugated leather backs, as if to match the airplane's skin. The floor is carpeted, and there is one seat on each side of the aisle. This early airliner has none of the cramped window space of so many modern-day aeronautical buses. Each window was built wide and the seats were set so that each passenger would have a panoramic view—except for the rearmost passengers.

Charles LeMaster has the psyche of a showman. To keep his Trimotor going, he must also have the acumen of a businessman. Keeping a Ford can be expensive. The tires wear out after 150 to 200 landings, however soft the touchdowns may be, and they cost five to six hundred dollars apiece. His insurance costs are tremendous. He has both passenger and public liability insurance and is restricted to carrying people just around the airport, sightseeing. He'll go to air shows anywhere and flies ten months out of the year.

The logistics of flying to an air show and making it pay can be tricky. He usually can give rides only when there are no other flight demonstrations, which means toward the beginning and end of each day. To cover his expenses, LeMaster charges air-show promoters a minimum show-up fee. He has no end of customers but sometimes has to give them their money back because he has run out of flying time.

The Ford Trimotor still has its mystique. At Pratt & Whitney's fiftieth-anniversary celebration in Hartford in 1976, the Trimotor was very popular. Some four hundred thousand people inspected the airplane in two days. LeMaster boasts that there was a path worn in the grass in the outline of his Ford Trimotor.

It takes a crew of four to operate the Trimotor at an air show or display: LeMaster and a copilot and two ground crew members—his wife, to sell the tickets and keep the books, and his son, acting as a

The LeMasters are the only folks around who have a Ford like this in their front yard. This silver beauty can be clearly seen from the highway, perched on top of a hill.

safety man, signaling his father during start-up to make up for the Ford's poor visibility when at rest. Even with all these people on hand, it would be a burden to hangar the airplane, considering all the flying it does; so it is left tied down on the top of a hill, next to LeMaster's twenty-seven-hundred-foot airstrip and ranch-style house in Ottawa. Passersby see the grand old airplane and stop to examine it. Many people have gone out of their way to see it.

The most poignant moments, however, come at the shows. A couple buy a ride because they were married in a Trimotor in 1929 and want to relive the memory. Another young couple has money for only one to ride, and the husband wants to put his wife aboard. LeMaster hustles them both inside: "When you get home, send me a check," he says. Old-timers come up to reminisce about Trimotors, one with a snapshot of that very airplane, when it had floats, being lowered into the Detroit River for its first flight.

The LeMasters are swept up in the humanity of it all. They are also swept up in some fame. They have given rides to the president of American Airlines and to astronaut Neil Armstrong. And they are swept up as if by a mission. "We're doing something good for the country," LeMaster says proudly, "because everybody likes airplanes." Kids are welcomed aboard and even at times allowed the pleasure of being copilot. Some older people stand in line just to talk with the LeMasters about old airplanes.

What they have is priceless—the airplane and the experience. Charles LeMaster buys and sells other airplanes, has owned airplanes since he was sixteen. That was in 1946, when he had a Stinson Voyager—which broke on takeoff and which he rebuilt himself. He knows the value of an airplane. Just one reason why, of many: at an air show, an admirer once asked a special favor of the LeMasters. He had an elderly lady friend who would like to be allowed to touch the Trimotor. He led the lady to the airplane. She reached out, touched it, and smiled her pleasure. The lady was blind.

LeMaster says, "I know some people who have airplanes they paid a million dollars for. I wouldn't trade mine for one of theirs."

Author's Note: The world of the antiquer constantly changes. For example, as we go to press, John Turgyan has sold his Howard DGA-15P, but only after purchasing an even rarer Howard, the last airworthy DGA-11. The DGA-11 is even more closely related to *Mister Mulligan;* it is sleeker, faster, and generally a better performer than the DGA-15P. He is treating his machine to a thorough and careful rebuild.

Charles LeMaster elected to sell his Ford Trimotor and buy a similar aircraft with better performance. His choice was the Bushmaster 2000. This aircraft was the result of an attempt started in the mid-fifties by a group of Californians to get an aircraft based on the Ford Trimotor back into production. Initially working with William Stout, who was responsible for the original Ford design and who unfortunately died in 1956 just as the project was getting under way, they succeeded in constructing a prototype that flew for the first time in August 1966.

The progression from prototype to production never transpired, however. The Bushmaster prototype did soldier on in Alaska, among other places, until it was purchased by LeMaster in 1977. LeMaster will barnstorm in it just as he did in the Ford.

LeMaster sold Ford Trimotor 414H to a subsidiary of Scenic Airlines in Las Vegas. There it joined a second Trimotor to be used for sightseeing flights over the city.

Scenic is a successful enterprise founded and developed by John Siebold, an astute and delightful gentleman. Scenic also flies commuter airliners on several routes in the Southwest and does air taxi and charter work.

II

A GALLERY OF CLASSICS

Dale Crites's 1910 Curtiss Pusher replica.

OVERLEAF
Wayne L. Amelang's 1930 Parks P2-A.

OPPOSITE
George Mennen's 1940 Spartan Executive.

This rare 1931 Bird CK is owned by Jeannie and Dick Hill and Russ Newhouse.

Phil Dacy in his 1940 Buecker Jungmeister.

A 1943 Beech D17-S Staggerwing of Don Hawkins in the sunset.

Alex (aft) and Marti (forward) in their 1929 Travel Air L-4000.

Loel Crawford in his 1941 Waco UPF-7.

A 1942 Lockheed C-60 Lodestar, owned by Jerry Walker and flown by Terry Boehler.

OPPOSITE
Gene Morris in his 1931 American Eaglet.

A PT-22 comes in at dusk at Blakesburg.

The Wasp Jr. on a Staggerwing roars to life.

The 1943 Cessna T-50 Bobcat of Gene Bottolfsen taxis by at Blakesburg.

III

HOW IT'S DONE

9

The Fine Art of Getting Started

GROUND RULES

Every restoration must be accomplished with attention to certain important considerations, which we will call ground rules.

Foremost among the ground rules are the legal considerations. The FAA requires that all restoration work on an aircraft be supervised by an A & P, an aircraft mechanic who holds federal licenses for aircraft and powerplant maintenance. This does not mean that you have to hire a mechanic to look over your shoulder every minute you are working on the restoration; it does mean that all major work on your antique must be checked by an A & P.

There is sometimes a problem in finding a properly qualified person. Even if a licensed mechanic is exceptionally knowledgeable about aviation's modern machines, it does not necessarily follow that he will also be familiar with a rare oldster; he will probably be the first to point this out. For this reason, it is a good idea to work through the antique clubs and to consult with owners of your aircraft type to find the right person for your particular project. Arrange an initial meeting with him to review your restoration plans, and discuss the specific problems—unusual engine types, fabric work, wing and fuselage repair, and so on—that he will have to check as your work progresses. Also, if a

OPPOSITE
Antiquer Bryce Hunt, at Santa Paula Airport in California, worked on his Howard DGA-15P for seven and a half years before his rebuild was done, one week before the 1978 Oshkosh fly-in.

financial arrangement is in order between you and the A & P, it would be a good idea to clarify the money details at this initial meeting, although it is not unusual to find someone willing to volunteer his assistance.

You should be aware that the FAA has precise specifications that must be met for each aircraft component that is to be repaired or rebuilt. Information on these specifications can be obtained from the appropriate FAA publication (see Bibliography), as well as from your local FAA representative.

Don Dickenson's hangar shop at Santa Paula Airport in southern California. A constant verbal exchange of information goes on among antiquers, since many important bits of information are not available in written form. The strange-looking object in the right foreground is a heater, hundreds of which are used in the nearby orange groves to help keep frost off the delicate citrus trees. A visit to Santa Paula is highly recommended for any antiquer. This airport is one of the "pockets" of heavy antique activity across the country. One of its most unusual features is that each hangar has its own gasoline storage tank. Dickenson, whose father founded the airport, owns two other antiques in addition to the Spartan.

It is also mandatory that an FAA representative inspect the restoration. One word of advice cannot be overemphasized: get the FAA representative involved from the beginning of the restoration and *before* you have covered up your fine workmanship.* Have him inspect at each milestone along the way, such as when you have completed the rebuilding of a major system or aircraft-component section.

If you fail to work with the FAA representative from the start, he is going to have some tough questions when you present him with a fait accompli. To satisfy him, you might have to undo work that has taken many tedious hours to accomplish. At the very worst, he could refuse to certify your ship as airworthy.

Remember that his job is to certify the *safety* of your aircraft; so a prudent antiquer cooperates with the FAA representative from the start of the restoration to its completion.

After you have pondered the FAA requirements, there are other important considerations to keep in mind. One of these is the question of tools.

Tool purchases can end up as one of the biggest expenditures in a restoration, especially if one must purchase a few power tools. However, quality tools will last a long time and can be used for a lot of things besides restoring aircraft. The frustration you avoid by having the correct tools to work with cannot be reckoned in dollars and cents, as any antiquer will testify.

Quality is not only a major consideration when purchasing tools; it is also most important when buying materials. Over and over again, antiquers stress that the wood, fabric, replacement parts, and other items you purchase for your restoration should be the best quality available. If they are not, it will show up sooner or later (usually sooner).

Also, it is better to replace a damaged part completely than to attempt repairing it. The best repair work is never as good as a complete replacement.

Finding quality materials is easier than locating suitable replacement parts. Stories abound among antiquers of searches—some lasting seven or eight years—for this or that part. Sometimes when a part is

---

*An A & P with the Aircraft Inspector rating can handle all inspections of a restored antique *if* the aircraft has a permanent Airworthiness Certificate. If not, then the FAA must inspect the aircraft and issue a *new* Airworthiness Certificate. Modifications during restoration can result in complicating the certification process no end.

Sometimes the search for a duplicate replacement part turns out to be fruitless and you have to come up with an acceptable substitute. You may not want to, but if it is the difference between flying and not flying, the dilemma is usually resolved in favor of the substitute. Charles LeMaster used oleos from a P-47, the Thunderbolt fighter of World War II, when he built up the main gear on his Ford, and . . .

... this wing tip is from a Grumman F4F-4 Wildcat fighter.

located after a long search, the prospective buyer discovers that the owner won't sell at any price! The Antique Airplane Association's Robert Taylor recounts that he spent two years looking for the proper-sized set of wheels for his 1929 General Aristocrat.

When the restoration is complete, the airplane may be comprised of parts of about five different airplanes—a situation not atypical in the antique restoration scene.

Almost every restoration project involves problems in locating appropriate replacement parts or materials. Again, the AAA aids its members by acting as a clearinghouse of information about where to obtain parts. The AAA estimates that it handles about five inquiries related to restoration problems per day.

Cleanliness conceivably ranks above the deities in restoration work. Every bit of wood and metal that undergoes rebuilding must first

LEFT
This is the aileron bellcrank section of one of the wings on Duane Golding's 1929 Brunner-Winkle Bird. One look can tell you that a rebuild is on the agenda. Golding keeps the old wings, however, to use as reference.

BELOW
Wayne Hayes needed to replace the fuel tank fitting on the right. It took him months to locate one, and when he finally did, he had to buy the whole fuel tank in order to get this one small fitting. This was not the first, nor will it be the last, time that an antiquer has had to go to extremes to get the replacement parts he needs.

be thoroughly cleaned. If it is not, it defeats the whole purpose of the restoration, since deterioration will continue instead of being arrested. Hidden rust will continue to oxidize metal, old dope deposits overlooked will keep new dope from adhering, and so on. Good preparation of the entire antique is as important as a quality rework job.

Each stage of the project should be carefully thought out in advance: what work is to be done? Who is going to do each specific job (you or a professional)? What combination of parts and tools will be used? Enough unanticipated hurdles will crop up as a matter of course without your having the additional worry of problems that could have been prevented—or at least anticipated—by early planning.

The antiquer can be up against systems in his aircraft that are as complex as any to be found. The retractable gear on this Beech Staggerwing is a good example. The aircraft originally appeared as a fixed-gear machine, and the retractable-gear feature was engineered in later as an afterthought. The result is a complicated group of bits of sheet-metal and tubing. Even bicycle chains help make up this system, which has been known to malfunction on more than one occasion. It is hard to keep clean and therefore hard to keep safe from corrosion. Reworking the gear on a Staggerwing can be one of those projects that first look as though they will take a couple of weeks but turn out to take months to finish.

This brings us to another cardinal rule concerning your restoration: take your time. One person cannot realistically expect to overcome the ravages of three or four decades in a few months. An average restoration will take about three years and then be perhaps only 95 percent complete. The remaining 5 percent may take another three years or longer. Projects that take five years or more are not at all unusual. Therefore, anyone considering taking on a restoration challenge must make a careful assessment of the length of his attention span. (It is assumed that he has already made a careful assessment of his pocketbook.)

A restoration is a big project—bigger than building your own airplane. Homebuilt aircraft constructors can at least begin with clean materials, whereas the antique restorer must first take his craft completely apart and prepare it for reconstruction. This entails clearing away accumulations of rust, dirt, dope, and the like. Homebuilders are not faced with the problems of finding replacement parts, either. If a homebuilt constructor wants a part he can't buy, he can make it himself from a standard design or even engineer his own solution by designing

Once in a while, you run across parts for your antique in the most unlikely places. Duane Golding of Sheboygan Falls, Wisconsin, ran across the original equipment wheels for his 1929 Brunner-Winkle Bird on a couple of wheelbarrows! He quickly made a deal with the owner, who had no idea of the rarity of these items.

The Stearman, looking into the aft end of its fuselage. The small pulley assembly at the top is part of the control cable system that leads to the tailfeathers. This system is one of the trickiest parts of the aircraft to rerig during a rebuild.

the part himself. An antiquer must sometimes search for years until he finds a satisfactory replacement part. He may never find an original.

During your self-examination, you will also want to take a long hard look at your competency in the skills that will be needed during the restoration. What is your manual-dexterity quotient? Can you operate power tools without endangering life and limb? Have you demonstrated such skills on previous projects, and have you undertaken projects that made similar demands on your patience and persistence?

There is a bright side to all of this. If you have never before taken on work of this kind, you are now leaving yourself open to a genuine education, as well as an enriching and broadening experience. You will have a chance to learn several different areas of aircraft work: fabric covering, metalwork, woodwork, and possibly engine work. All that knowledge about your own aircraft will help you to maintain it better, and it will encourage you to use your plane more often and with greater confidence. You'll know that if a time comes when you are in the middle of nowhere with a maintenance problem, your hard-won know-

Many antiques are made up of substantial portions of different materials, so that the restorer must familiarize himself with the techniques of working with fabric, sheet metal, wood, and other materials. In this photo of John Turgyan's Howard, the beginning of the fabric portion of the fuselage can be seen at right, while the sheet metal surrounding the cabin, fairings, and other portions is also visible. Over a dozen pieces of sheet metal can be seen in this one area.

how will help you to cope with the situation with the skill of a professional.

Finally, if you decide to take up the challenge, it is a good idea to program yourself. Set up your own deadlines so that every few months you have something substantial to show for your efforts. In this way, you will avoid becoming discouraged. Taking care of your mental health is never mentioned in the technical guidebooks, but it is just as important as careful workmanship. It can mean the difference between proud accomplishment and simply giving up.

Every antiquer will tell you that the sense of accomplishment after the job is complete is something that simply cannot be put into words. It is a feeling that antiquers communicate to each other with a smile or an understanding nod. There is a proud bond between them. Again and again, you will hear them say, "You really don't know how much hard work goes into a restoration until you've tried it yourself." Interestingly, after an antiquer finishes his first restoration, he almost always begins another.

Walter Ballard, eighty-two, is supervisor of restoration for the San Diego Aero-Space Museum. Here he stands in front of a World War I Jenny. He and several other volunteer workers completed restoration of the machine only four months before it was destroyed in the museum's fire, which occurred approximately six hours after this photo was taken. Ballard is holding one of two pairs of leaf springs from a truck, which he used to make the louvers on the engine cowling. He would first clamp a pair of springs on each side of the louver area, then carefully chisel the long cut in the sheet metal, using the aft set of springs as a guide. Using a contoured block of wood and a mallet, he then pounded out the louver form. When the result was to his satisfaction, he detached the aft set of springs and moved it forward, leaving enough space for the next louver between the two pairs of springs, and repeated the chiseling and metal-forming process.

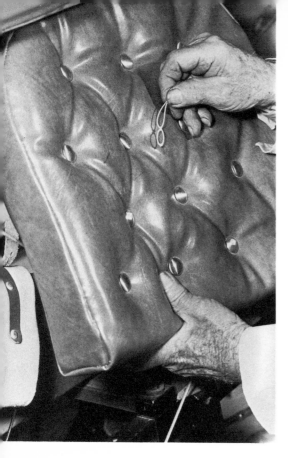

The two sides of the seat cushion on the Jenny are identical. In order to make the buttons draw the upholstery down evenly on each side, Ballard first took a length of string about six inches long and secured a button to the middle with a square knot. Then he tied a second square knot about an inch away from the first, as shown. He did exactly the same thing to all fourteen buttons used on one side of the cushion. Next, he inserted the string through the upholstery with a needle in the proper position, tying another button on the opposite side as he progressed. Naturally, the second button could go down only as far as the second square knot, and since each pair of knots was evenly spaced, the result was even spacing all across the cushion.

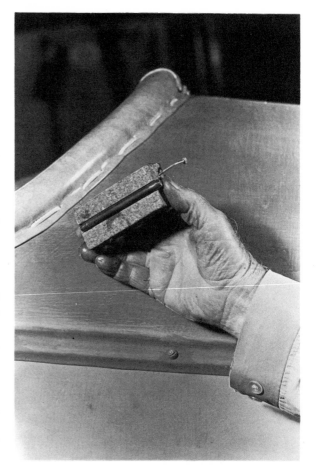

On the bottom of the turtledeck under Ballard's wrist and on portions of the engine cowling are ridges called beading, made in the metal by Ballard in the following manner: He first took a small block of hardwood and drilled a hole through its length. This hole was the diameter of a rod from an engine. He then sawed the block lengthwise and glued the rod into one of the channels. A nail pounded into each end and bent around allowed the block with the rod in it to be held firmly in a vise. The sheet metal was laid over the rod and the other block with the channel laid over that. The top block was then struck with a mallet and the metal guided through the two blocks to form the beading. An additional piece of wood (not shown) was nailed to the side of the block with the rod in it and used as a stop when the metal was slipped over the rod.

The windscreen on the Jenny was originally
fitted to the fuselage with a piece of sheet
metal formed at an angle and running all
around the bottom edge of the screen. In
lieu of this metal piece, which is not easy to
form, Ballard elected to use the small metal
tabs shown here.

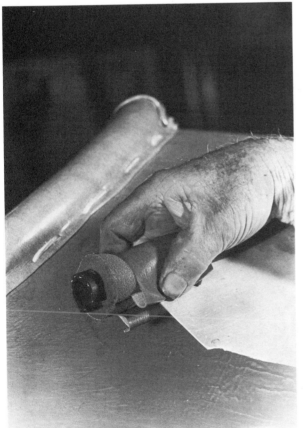

Here Ballard demonstrates how he formed
the padding around the rim of the cockpits.
The foundation of the padding is made of
washer drain hose slit along its length. The
hose is surrounded by foam, its edges
tucked into the slit in the hose. This in turn
is covered by naugahyde upholstery that has
its edges folded under and glued to provide
a double thickness for the stitching of
rawhide that secures the padding to the
fuselage. The original was formed in a more
tedious manner—alternately stuffed with
horsehair and sewn to the cockpit edge a
few inches at a time.

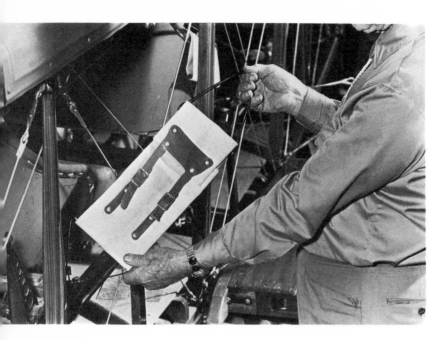

Following a tradition of improvisation established by the barnstormers of yore, Ballard fashioned this safety belt for the Jenny from an old U.S. Mail bag.

INSPECTION AND MOVING

Unless your rational faculties were completely overwhelmed when you bought your vintage airplane—a condition not uncommon to antique addicts—you probably gleaned some notion of its airworthiness during your prepurchase inspection. Now is the time to conduct a thorough, merciless examination of what is required in the way of restoration.

First check the notations in the logbooks (if you have them) for warning clues about the maintenance problems of your particular aircraft. Former owners, and owners of the same aircraft type, will be able—even eager—to give you the benefit of their experience. The publications of aircraft-type clubs and factory manuals will provide a comprehensive picture of the way things ought to be. This homework should be done before you begin any detailed inspection of your antique.

If you do not have all the records pertaining to your particular aircraft, or suspect that you do not, you should contact the Records Division of the FAA in Oklahoma City (see Appendix), and they will provide you with copies of all the records they have on your aircraft. The cost is nominal; you need only submit your registration number, name, and address.*

It may be accurate to say that any accumulation of parts that was once an airplane can be repaired by someone. The question you must ask yourself is this: is that someone me? To help answer it, remember that old hands in the game say that a good way to estimate the time and money involved in a restoration is to take your most exaggerated guess, multiply it by three—and then add a year and a thousand dollars for good measure.

With that in mind, it must be remembered that the inspection and ultimately the dismemberment of your airplane is a lesson in patience. As we are often told in the case of an accident victim, a hasty move in the interest of assisting the patient may simply worsen the situation. Inspection of your airplane must proceed in a careful, methodical way. It is wise to make notes and drawings as you uncover areas that have not been looked at for decades.

In the case of most antiques you can assume that the fabric must be replaced, so it will be in order to cut small inspection holes in the old fabric on the fuselage and wings to examine the condition of the skeleton. In most wooden structures, it is prudent to take a pessimistic view of many of the small interior braces. Metal frames and stringers may be returned to service, but they must all be examined and tested before they can be relied on.

Acting as your own A & P, you will make notes on all findings during your inspection tour. If you can have someone familiar with the aircraft type (preferably a licensed mechanic) perform the inspection with you, so much the better.

A veritable gold mine of information about what to look for can be found in the profusely illustrated FAA publication *Personal Aircraft Inspection Handbook* (see Appendix). No aircraft owner should be without a copy. With the *Handbook,* you don't have to be a professional to recognize much of what needs to be repaired or replaced. The secret is to know where to look and what to look for.

---

*The records will include copies of all "form 337s" filled out on your particular aircraft. These forms are completed by mechanics who have made major repairs or alterations to it. See Appendix, page 245.

Sometimes blueprints for the rebuild are impossible to come by. Duane Golding found a helpful substitute in a model airplane publication that had detailed, blueprintlike drawings that matched his 1929 Brunner-Winkle Bird.

You will also discover that structural failure and wear occur predominantly at joints where one thing meets another. This is true of welds, wires, hinges, cables, and everything else. It is especially true where two dissimilar materials come into contact and where any kind of movement, intentional or unintentional, takes place. These facts hold true for vintage planes as much as they do for the more modern aircraft pictured in the *Handbook*.

The *Handbook* also lists the tools you will need to undertake an inspection.

After the initial triumph of finding one's antique and concluding the sale, the crucial hurdle facing the antique owner is getting his acquisition home safely—especially if, as usually happens, the plane is not in flying condition. Many rare and irreplaceable aircraft have been damaged or destroyed in shipment, even when the transfer was made by professional movers. Moving old airplanes is an art that requires prior planning. As in flying cross-country, careful planning results in the ability to cope with the unexpected and, eventually, in a safe and successful journey. Seeking the assistance of an experienced plane

AAA volunteers construct a framework to hold the wing on top of the flatbed. Small blocks are nailed by Wayne Hayes to the framework to keep the wing from shifting transversely during transit. The wing was one of many antique aircraft parts donated to the Airpower Museum of the Antique Airplane Association by Mrs. Joseph Moro in memory of her late husband. Careful planning resulted in the safe transfer of this wing and many other components from New Jersey to Blakesburg.

Wayne Hayes (left) and Jim Thomas secure the wing to the temporary framework built on top of the long flatbed. They loop strong nylon cord around the framework and the wing's spars.

mover will also give you an edge; moving an antique plane is not easily done by one person.

Mitch Mayborn of Dallas moved his Ryan STM-S2 fifteen hundred miles from California on a trailer.* After an original estimate from a professional household mover was increased from $450 to $1,600, he decided to take charge of the move himself. Before he left, he worked everything out on paper, down to an hour-by-hour trip plan. He was also lucky enough to have the assistance of G. "Andy" Anderson, a retired pilot, who understood the intricacies of moving aircraft.

Mayborn used his 1961 Studebaker pickup to tow the trailer. He took along a few extra parts for the truck—generator, starter, fuel pump, and water pump. As Mayborn later related, "We needed the generator, and we lost only about thirty minutes changing it. Planning paid off."

He made a checklist. He felt he would have to monitor the truck and trailer closely, since he planned to drive straight through with no overnight stops. An antique plane sitting naked on a trailer in a motel parking lot, he figured, might attract some unwanted attention. The checklist covered gas, oil, windows, lights, hoses, V-belts, tires (both truck and trailer), tiedowns, tarps, hitch, and gear fluid.

Mayborn solicited the advice of others who had taken their antiques over the same route he planned to travel. For example, E. M. Johnson, Jr., state director of the Automobile Association of America in Texas, warned him of the high winds at Banning Pass, between San Bernardino and Palm Springs—information that road maps don't relay. And after consulting with the auto club, Mayborn was able to pinpoint areas en route where roads were under construction.

Mayborn selected a tandem-wheel trailer because it offers more stability and safety in case of a blowout at highway speeds. He had to search around for a while before he found one that would do the job. The biggest U-Haul model available was not suitable. He finally found a satisfactory set of wheels at a local filling station.

Mayborn then did a bit of sketching, taking the dimensions of the aircraft from a three-view and roughing them onto a sketch of the trailer. The engine was to be crated and would ride over the rear axle of the pickup. The rest of the space on the pickup bed and in the trailer was mapped out like the floor plan of a house. Each component was listed

*See his excellent article describing this experience in the AAA publication *Antique Airplane News*, for the second quarter of 1975.

and planned for in advance—wings, control surfaces, tail feathers, wheel fairings, etc. The list was used when the components were loaded on the trailer and truck so that nothing was left behind—an embarrassing and frustrating experience that has befallen more than one antiquer.

Mayborn, with Anderson's help, was able to get everything onto his pickup and trailer. "The load didn't fit exactly as planned, but the drawings and lists made a big difference in speed of loading since we knew what we had to do and we had planned a sequence."

The aircraft was to ride nose forward, and it would be rolled up the front of the trailer tail first on tracks Mayborn had installed on the trailer bed. "I knew the wheel tread of the Ryan, and put down two-by-twelve tracks. I welded a mount onto the front of the trailer so that when we lowered that end to the ground, the two-by-twelve made a good ramp. By preplanning, I knew that when we rolled the airplane up the ramp, we would have to stop midway and remove the spreader bar between the gear legs to clear the trailer's jack, located just aft of the hitch. The jack extends up from the hitch about a foot when the front of the trailer is resting on the ground.

"We would then have to push the aircraft up the ramp a few more inches, replace the spreader bar, and continue to move the fuselage and gear assembly onto the bed of the trailer. It's much better to know in advance so you can do this than to be suddenly confronted with the problem in the middle of the loading process."

Mayborn suggests that anyone planning a do-it-yourself move should take these items along:

- tarpaulins (both canvas and plastic)
- rope—at least 200 feet of quarter-inch, and 100 feet of half-inch
- duct tape—a big roll ("We used it for everything from holding the truck together to covering the plexiglass on the plane.")
- loading ramp (must be custom-made for your aircraft)
- block and tackle
- hammer, nails, and boards
- any other tools you might need; extra gas cans
- old mattresses, used for padding. ("We got these for two dollars each at a used-mattress store. They were awfully dirty and I hated to touch them, but they kept the aircraft components from being damaged during the trip. Throw them away when you get home.")

The Ryan arrived at its new home with no damage, after a four-day journey that included a 4:00 A.M. breakdown when the left wheel bearing gave out on the Studebaker, right in the middle of nowhere in West Texas. Despite twenty-knot winds at 30° F, Anderson stayed with the aircraft and disabled truck as Mayborn hoofed it to a gas station a few miles back. Mayborn carried with him the key to finding the correct replacement bearing—the service manual for the truck—confirming once again the value of thorough advance planning.

A few more tips. When you take the aircraft apart for loading, make notes on the position of each item or assembly, including how it was attached before removal. You might even take before-and-after photographs. As each component is secured to the truck or trailer, be sure that each of the places where a component is going to be subjected to stress or vibration is padded enough to keep it from bending, breaking, or getting damaged in any way.

If the prop is exposed, it should be lashed to keep it from windmilling. The wings should also be lashed and positioned in a fashion that will keep them from flying away—also something that a few antiquers have learned from hard experience. If a piece of your load flies off your rig, it might wreck the component, or even cause a serious accident for which you could be held liable.

The legal-width highway traffic limitations of each state you plan to drive through should be checked to assure that your load will not exceed the limit.

Moving an antique aircraft involves more than simply throwing a few parts in the back of a truck; indeed, it involves some of the most accident-prone time you will spend with your aircraft. But if you plan your move carefully, you will reduce the amount of risk and unexpected delays to a minimum. Further, you will feel well rewarded for the time spent in planning, when your vintage plane sits safely at last on home ground. Then you will be ready to begin restoring it to flying condition.

A good working area and good tools are valuable conveniences. But although not everyone has them or can afford them, it is possible to do excellent work even under adverse conditions. Generally, we have to settle for what we can get, and it works out well enough.

The location of a shop depends on your work habits. If you want to put in a couple of hours every evening, then a shop at home is practically a necessity unless your domestic situation can tolerate being away

A good selection of the right tools is essential. Here, Don Dickenson has removed the gear of his Spartan Executive in order to have the O rings in the gear struts replaced.

every night and weekends too. If you plan to work only on weekends, a shop in a hangar at an airport (or elsewhere where space can be rented) might be better in many ways. For instance, 220-volt electric power is more likely to be available in a rented shop space than in a home garage. A rented space also produces fewer conflicts with other activities—the use of a garage for cars, for instance.

Some kind of temperature control is helpful. For gluing and doping, correct temperature and humidity are important, and if you don't have some way of controlling them, you are at the mercy of the weather. Good lighting is cheap and very valuable, even if it takes a few days to rig it up. A powerful shop vacuum cleaner will become important when the cleaning and sawing and sanding begin.

A large working surface, at least four by eight feet (and preferably twice that), can be built of shop-grade plywood; take care to make it

By using sawhorses that are about chest high, Wayne Hayes spares himself an aching back while rubbing out the finish on the wings of his Waco. Hayes uses his spare time during the winter to bring the components of his aircraft home to work on in the comfort of his garage. This way, he says, he can work for a while, take a break, answer the phone, and so on, arranging the time he has to work on the aircraft around the time he must spend on his two jobs.

sturdy and level. The sawhorses should not make bending uncomfortable. Sawhorses usually have to be built, as the ones used by carpenters for sawing are too low. Depending on the type of work you are doing, various sorts of frames or jigs may be better than horses. Wings, for instance, are often set up in vertical frames so that the two sides are easily accessible; also, twist is readily measured with plumb bobs in such a frame. A fuselage might be set up on a couple of trunnions turning in wooden V-blocks so that it can be rotated easily. For welding flat tubular structures, the flat tabletop is a sufficient jig. (The work may be set clear of the table on blocks to prevent burning the table during tacking; alternatively, a separate piece of plywood with locating blocks nailed to the surface is used for tacking and is discarded later.)

People use anything from a single crate to dozens of baby-food jars for storing miscellaneous small hardware. Jars are rather inconvenient, especially for mixed nuts and the like, since you have to open them, pour out the contents, study them, and then put the whole works back inside just to find one part. Open cardboard parts trays are better, but in a shop where woodworking is done they have the disadvantage of collecting sawdust. Hinged covers of thin plywood folding down over rows of trays solve this problem; it all depends on how fancy you feel like getting.

Don't be in too much of a hurry to equip your shop. Get some basic tools and do some basic jobs; the longer you work, the more time you'll have to come across good bargains and the more you'll learn from fellow antiquers about the best tools to use. Good tools do good work, however, so don't put off getting the necessities, like a drill press and handsaw. Used tools are fine if they work all right and if replacement parts are available.

Hobbyists often omit some of the refinements of good shop procedure, ultimately to their regret. For instance, drill bits ought to be sharpened often for good results; you can easily learn to do this by hand, or get a small jig to make it still easier. A medium-sized grinder that will not bog down under load is a necessity from the beginning, for various sharpening jobs among other things. A supply of fresh hacksaw blades of various types saves a lot of trouble, as does lots of fresh sandpaper and proper cutting oils for drilling, tapping, and fly-cutting (kerosene or solvent for aluminum, heavier oil for steels). All cutting and grinding operations are much easier and produce much more satisfactory results when performed with fresh edges and at the correct speeds and pressures; but hobbyists, out of a misguided sense of economics, often labor along with dull blades and exhausted sandpaper. Professionals, by contrast, make things easy for themselves by discarding materials sooner. What they lose in this way they regain in time and effort saved. The moral: follow the practices of the professionals and don't skimp. This is also good advice when it comes to selecting tools.

It is almost always wise to avoid the least expensive tools, unless you want to use them only once. There are a few exceptions. Inexpensive variable-speed electric drill motors will give long service if they are not overtaxed; but you may find that you need a more powerful, more expensive one to fall back on for heavy work. In that case, you might as well just get the more expensive one in the first place.

Multipurpose tools such as drill presses that clamp a hand drill or fittings that turn drill motors into power saws or belt sanders are usually

Problem solving in the shop. Don Dickenson found that the pitot tube on his Spartan was an eye-level hazard. A couple of rubber chickens turned something dangerous into something droll.

not a good bet. Well-aligned holes are important in an aircraft; inexpensive drill presses do not have the necessary precision. There are a few expensive multipurpose tools that are well made and last a long time while doing what you want them to do, but most of the lightly built economy models end up in the trash after a little while.

Speaking of trash, a large trash container is a great help, as is the courage to throw things into it. Once in a while you may regret having thrown some piece of scrap away, but usually the mess produced by saving everything is worse than the occasional regret.

Although good work can be done in cramped, messy quarters, and successful projects have emerged from the most unlikely places (often, skilled or meticulous workmen surround themselves with appalling disorder, with no apparent ill effects), you should start off at least by trying to use the right tool for each job. Experienced workmen may learn to escape the consequences of ignoring this rule, but a beginner should adhere to it. Do not try to make one crescent wrench do the work of a set of box wrenches or sockets; do not apply one screwdriver indiscriminately to instruments and axles. Buy quality sets of wrenches, sockets, screwdrivers, and nut drivers. Do not use a penknife as a gear puller. People who would not think of eating salad with a pitchfork may be found doing comparable things in their workshops with tools and parts.

If your work will involve riveting or painting, you will need an air compressor. The bigger the better, preferably with a pressure switch and a regulator. This may represent an investment of two or three hundred dollars, or you may scrounge one, or build one for less, using such parts as water-heater tanks and refrigerator compressors and motors.

A good source for some types of tools is newspapers, garage sales, and swap meets. Some tools, such as a large bench vise, C-clamps, brushes and chisels, hammers or mallets, crowbars, and so on, are not likely to be much the worse for years of use. Files require critical inspection; if worn or rusted they are not worth much.

Things like files are cheap and handy, and it's good to have a lot of different sizes, shapes, and teeth; so you may as well buy any likely candidates you come across at bargain prices. Small-and medium-sized paint brushes are also good to collect, as are rags; they are often easier to throw away than to clean.

If children may gain access to your work area (and they gain access to everything, eventually), you should have a locker or padlocked chest in which to store paints, solvents, and such dangerous fluids as MEK and parts cleaner. In using those fluids you should, for your own safety, have a good source of ventilation such as a powerful exhaust fan *and* a place for fresh air to come in. It is also wise to stock up on safety items such as ear defenders (for use when bandsawing sheet metal, for instance), safety goggles, and filter inhalators for paint spraying and working with substances like fiberglass or foam plastics. Usually, people neglect to get those items, and then when the time comes to use them, they resolve to get them tomorrow, working without in the meantime. It is much more sensible to get them in advance, to have spares—preferably separate protective garb conveniently placed near each tool that might require it—and to force yourself into the habit of using them always.

Tools and equipment are expensive; a well-supplied shop adds up to an investment comparable in importance to the airplane itself. For most people, however, the investment in shop equipment is much less satisfying emotionally than investments in airplane parts, so they avoid getting certain tools and depend on loans for others. There's no great harm in that (everybody does it), but sometimes it's a waste of time and effort to save money that way. The reasonable approach is to do some

Nothing unusual in an antiquer's household: a study becomes a temporary parts-storage warehouse in the Hayes's home.

The search for perfection: John Turgyan cuts new sheet metal for a replacement cowling to fit his Howard DGA-15P. The fit on the cowling, although acceptable to the casual observer, did not satisfy Turgyan, who elected to replace it completely.

basic planning and equipping *before* putting the airplane into the shop—setting up benches, lights, and ventilation, for instance. Then, when you actually begin your work, devote the necessary effort to building fixtures and stands to hold things in convenient positions for working. (This step isn't indispensable, but usually you're glad you did it afterward.) Then, and only then, start working on the plane, acquiring the necessary specialized tools as you go along. At first, the expenses of shop equipment will seem disproportionately large, but later you will lack fewer and fewer things. By spreading out your purchases of tools, you avoid the unnecessary items, stand a better chance of finding good deals, and soften the fiscal blow.

The appearance of a shop is unimportant. The tastes and inclinations of different workers vary widely, and it is pointless to try to imitate someone else's impeccable neatness if you are a naturally disorderly person. All that matters is the final product. There everyone should strive for the same thing: perfection.

The Wasp Jr. powerplant is one of the most popular engines among antiquers. Based on a mid-twenties design, this Pratt & Whitney engine has powered seventy different aircraft, several of which are still flying today as part of the antique movement. They include this Spartan 7W of Don Dickenson, based at Santa Paula, California, the Howard DGA-15P described in chapter 2, the Ford Trimotor in chapter 8, some Staggerwing Beeches, some Stearmans, the last surviving Douglas Dolphin, the Vultee Valiant, some Cabin Wacos, and several other designs, including various Lockheed Twins of the thirties. It has a reputation for being smooth-running and very reliable, and for having an ability to consume enormous quantities of gas and oil. There are a few shops in the United States that make a business out of rebuilding these engines, and they are patronized by the many antiquers who have a Wasp or two up front. A total of 39,027 Wasp Jr.'s were manufactured.

10

Powerplants

ANTIQUE AIRPLANE ENGINES

From our present vantage point we incline to assume that early aircraft engines must have been primitive. Starting with this prejudice, it is interesting to look through old books on aero engines—there are many of them dating from the teens and twenties—and see what a wealth of startling ideas and realizations there was, how ingenious many of them were, and how refreshingly different from the monotonously similar engines available today. It may be that the horizontal-opposed, air-cooled engines that power all modern light aircraft are somehow superior to every alternative, but when you see how many alternatives there are, you wonder whether the ascendancy of the flat-opposed engine was really historically inevitable. More likely, economic reasons brought it into prominence, and the demise of all but a few engine manufacturers kept it there.

Around the turn of the century, when the problem of providing powerplants for aircraft became urgent, engines—or prime movers, as they were often called—customarily weighed as much as 100 or 200 pounds per horsepower. Airplanes, however, required powerful engines of light weight, which nevertheless cooled satisfactorily and had a low vibration level (since the mass of the entire airframe was, in many cases, only a little greater than that of the engine).

Initially, engine development took several different paths. There were liquid-cooled and air-cooled designs, the latter inherently lighter but more prone to overheat at low forward speeds. Liquid-cooled

/ 143

engines had been widely used in cars, and generally they presented a smaller frontal area to the wind. They were also more complex than air-cooled ones. These considerations—the smaller frontal area of the liquid-cooled engine versus the simplicity and lightness of the air-cooled engine—persisted through World War II, when the rivalry between liquid- and air-cooled engines was still under way, and the question was rendered moot only by the arrival of turbines. After World War II, liquid-cooled engines were supplanted in light aircraft by air-cooled ones, and no liquid-cooled light aircraft engines were manufactured. Today, liquid-cooled engines based on automotive designs are again being used experimentally in some light airplanes.

The layouts of the original liquid-cooled engines were the familiar ones—in line, inverted in-line, and V-block. There were also liquid-cooled radials that combined the excessive weight of one type with the excessive frontal area of the other. The best known of the early liquid-cooled engines was the Curtiss OX-5, a 90-hp, 377-pound V-8 that originally powered the famous Jenny, among others. Many OX-5s were manufactured, and though they were eventually supplanted in most

The look of determination on Ralph Driscoll's face is nothing unusual. You have to have plenty of determination to restore an airplane as old as this 1928 Waco 10. You need even more of it to keep its OX-5 engine running, because an OX-5 was never one of aviation's most reliable powerplants. Everything has to revolve around you as the owner. When the engine isn't running right, what do you do? Take it to your local A & P? How much experience do you think he has had with an OX-5? Most antique owners are in the same boat, because the only mechanics who ever worked on OX-5s regularly are dead by now; ergo, it is up to you.

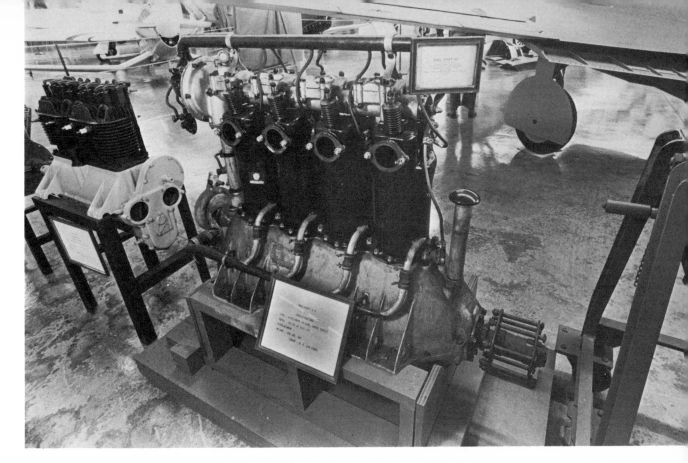

This water-cooled Hall-Scott L4 engine is in the Experimental Aircraft Association Museum at Franklin, Wisconsin. It generated 125 hp at 1,650 rpm and weighed 350 pounds dry. It was donated to the museum by the U.S. Air Force.

applications by the Hispano-Suiza, or "Hisso" (of about the same weight but much more powerful and reliable), they lived on in displays in trade schools and libraries, and also in a lot of three-seat biplanes that proliferated after World War I, feeding on the supply of surplus OX-5s. Many of the surviving engines were scrapped during World War II. Those that remain today are but a tiny fraction of the original production.

It was common for a given airframe to carry, at one time or another, any of five or six types of engines. A typical post–World War I biplane might have started its career with a surplus OX-5 that had been built by any of a series of auto manufacturers, or later by the Wright Aeronautical Company, which was eventually to dominate a large portion of the market with a series of highly reliable radial engines. The liquid-cooled OX-5 might have been replaced by a Hisso or by an in-line Hall-Scott, and that in turn, at one time or another, by a Wright J-5, Warner Scarab, Curtiss Challenger, or Axelson.

One of the most outlandish engine types from the early days, the one that most astonishes the modern eye, is the rotary. Combinations of gears, cams, cranks, and rods were tried in bewildering variety before World War I, and though many types of engines—floating-piston designs, for instance, and so-called axial radials—quickly became defunct, rotaries played an important role in the aircraft of World War I. Several varieties were tried, the essential idea being that of securing something other than the crankcase and cylinders to the airframe in such a way that the entire radially arranged engine was allowed to turn while the crankshaft (or in some exotic instances some third shaft or carriage) was fixed. The idea was to provide flywheel effect, air cooling, and some centrifugal supercharging effect without any weight penalty whatever; and astonishing as it seems today, the idea worked. Rotaries were mechanically very simple, the most ingenious versions (the so-called monosoupapes, from the French for single valves) using the crankcase for a carburetor of sorts, providing mixture intake by means of ported pistons as well as a single exhaust valve that also let air *in*, thus eliminating most of the moving parts of the reciprocating engine.

Rotaries, some of which were astonishingly large, capable of delivering up to 200 hp, had disadvantages that were eventually to make them extinct. One, from the pilot's standpoint, was the gyroscopic effect produced by the large rotating mass at the front of the airplane, which made it difficult in certain cases to maneuver satisfactorily. Because of the problems of carburetion in a rotating engine, rotaries were not throttled; they were controlled by cutting the ignition in and out. Either the engine was running flat out or it was freewheeling.* Centrifugal forces tended to tear the ignition wires loose. Unburned castor oil spewed from the cylinder heads along with the deafening, unmuffled exhaust, bathing all behind until cowlings were developed, which collected all the exhaust and oil and let it escape through a large gap at the bottom. Rotaries were also likely to catch fire.

Despite these inconveniences, some of them quite serious, a number of famous World War I fighters were powered with light, powerful rotary engines, and the names *Gnome* and *Le Rhône* still have a familiar sound.

With improvements in metallurgy and refinements in cylinder

---

*World War I aircraft restoration expert Cole Palen and his friends are able to fly rotary-powered aircraft *in formation*—no mean accomplishment.

This Gnome rotary engine powered Billy Parker's Pusher, now suspended from the ceiling in the Tulsa Airport Terminal.

design, it became increasingly possible to cool cylinders satisfactorily without recourse either to liquids or to such extraordinary devices as spinning the entire engine. The fixed-case, turning-crank engine, whatever its shortcomings compared with the rotary, was in the long run more tractable, efficient, and dependable; and by 1930, air-cooled radial engines were capable of delivering 1 horsepower for 1.5 pounds of weight.

An early problem of radial design was that of oil running down past piston seals into the bottom pistons while the engine was stationary. To avoid this, some very early designs—for example, the three-cylinder Anzani that powered Blériot across the English Channel in 1909—were actually fan-shaped. Such an arrangement is unbalanced, however, and requires heavy crankshaft counterweights to prevent vibration. The axially symmetrical form was preferable, and means of preventing oil from flowing into the bottom cylinders during idle periods were quickly found. The power-to-weight ratios of radial engines dropped rapidly during the twenties, from nearly 4 lb/hp for a LeBlond 60 (65 hp) to 1.5 lb/hp for a Wright Cyclone (525 hp). Reliability also increased rapidly, as was demonstrated convincingly (if not conclusively) by Lindbergh's 1927 Atlantic crossing in a Wright J-5-powered design based on the Ryan Brougham.

Although air-cooled radial engines existed from the early days of aviation, the "modern" radial was the result of the work of Charles L. Lawrence, a former navy officer who, with navy encouragement, investigated the possibilities of air-cooled radials of substantial power output. Lindbergh's Wright J-5 was the result of Lawrence's work, for which he was awarded the Collier Trophy in 1927.*

Many of the early radials are still flying on restorations today. There is the Detroit Air-Cat, a five-cylinder, 75-hp engine that was installed on the first Monocoupe and became the basis for the 60-hp Velie engine, which was standard on series-production Monocoupes through 1931. The Velie, in turn, inspired the 90-hp Lambert, which powered some later Monocoupes and which in its turn gave way to 125-hp Warner and Kinner engines. It was only at the beginning of the

*The Collier Trophy, named after the New York publisher of the famous magazine that bore his name, has been awarded annually since 1912 for "the greatest achievement in aviation in America, the value of which has been thoroughly demonstrated during the preceding year." The award is presented by the National Aeronautic Association, formerly the Aero Club of America. This award was originally called the Aero Club of America Trophy, but in 1944, twenty-six years after the death of its donor, its name was changed.

OPPOSITE
George Mennen lands his Wasp-powered Spartan Executive.

One reason to have kids is that you will have someone to clean up your aircraft. This is "Doc" Lindquist's Stearman, which has a big Lycoming for a nose. A smooth and accomplished pilot, Doc competes in aerobatic contests for antiquers with this machine. This handsome and genteel gentleman also has a Bonanza, which he uses to take his family all around the country. His wife flies a tiny Rose Parrakeet, which is painted yellow, like the Stearman, and is called, naturally, the *Yellow Rose*. One of this couple's favorite sports is to arrive at a fly-in in formation. The pilots and their airplanes live in Kansas City.

This Wright J4B Whirlwind engine has been sectioned so that a visitor to the EAA Museum can closely examine its inner workings.

forties that manufacturers of Monocoupes, which had dominated the lightplane scene for a decade, switched from radials to less costly Lycoming and Franklin flat-opposed engines.

The Warner Scarab, a seven-cylinder engine weighing 270 pounds and developing 110 hp (and later 125 hp), is still a favorite among antiquers today because of its smoothness and reliability; it is found on Monocoupe Model 90 AWs, a few Ryan SCWs (used 145- and 165-hp models), and on the Cessna Airmasters, which used 145- and 165-hp versions of the engine.

This Cessna Airmaster of Gar Williams has a Warner Scarab engine, as do many of its contemporaries from the thirties. Williams is head of the Airmaster Club and has one of the finest examples of the type. The Airmaster is one of the most aesthetically pleasing aircraft ever designed. Its clean lines provide exceptionally good performance for the amount of horsepower available—150 mph cruise on 145 hp—and it has been called the world's most efficient airplane. The Airmaster is an outgrowth of the second design Clyde Cessna made on his own after he split with Walter Beech. (Beech, Clyde Cessna, and Lloyd Stearman had headed up the Travel Air Company, which produced biplanes, including the one described in chapter 5). Cessna wanted to build a monoplane with a cantilever wing, and Beech, among others, thought he was wrong, so Cessna formed his own company. Cessna's first plane had a 120-hp Anzani, and the second (from which the production machines were developed, including Williams's) had a 110-hp Warner. Variations on this basic design put the company solidly into the lightplane business.

The Rearwin Company acquired the LeBlond engine designs (five- and seven-cylinder radials) in 1938, renamed them *Ken-Royce*, after the two Rearwin brothers, and installed them on Sportsters and Cloudsters (the earlier Model 6000M Speedsters had used in-line Cirrus and Menasco engines); but eventually, again, the radials were supplanted by flat-opposed Franklins and Continentals after 1940.

One also encounters on very small aircraft, such as the American Eaglet, Curtiss Junior, or some early Cubs, the three-cylinder, 40-hp Szekely engine (incorrectly but commonly pronounced Sickly), which was a troublesome one that did not go far. (One notable recent exception has been the Szekely on the 1931 American Eaglet of Gene and Mary Morris of Hampshire, Illinois.)

This 36-hp 1931 Aeronca E-113C restored by Pete Springer and Vic Warnock in 1972 was one of the first horizontally opposed aircraft engine designs. It was one of the powerplants used on the Aeronca C-3 airframe, a popular, low-cost lightplane of the early thirties. This example was part of the San Diego Aero-Space Museum collection.

A Pratt & Whitney radial powers this Staggerwing Beech—seen here arriving at Atchison, Kansas, home of Amelia Earhart. The Wasp was the most popular engine for this design, which is considered by many to be the Cadillac of antique aircraft. Its unusual appearance makes it stand out in any gathering of aircraft, and its performance statistics are as good as those of any single-engine, high-performance retractable built today. But when it comes to economy. . .

In the early thirties, the precursors of modern engines appeared in the form of opposed two-cylinder Aeroncas of 20 and 36 hp or so. A few of these are still flying. They were soon followed by four-cylinder flat engines of 40 and then 65 hp, which gained immense popularity on the ubiquitous Taylor/Piper Cub. The day of the radial was ending. Although World War II saw the continued use in combat aircraft both of big radials of up to 3,000 hp and of V-block liquid-cooled designs with somewhat less power, and although radials continue today in airline and agricultural service in many parts of the world, the war put a sudden end to the use of radials in light aircraft—and, coincidentally, to the era of the aircraft that today are considered "antique."

ENGINE OVERHAUL

As in almost every other aspect of restoration, a licensed mechanic must at least approve the work done on the engine—that is, he must "sign it off." If the engine is of a modern type, a horizontal-opposed engine in the Contoming tradition, then any powerplant mechanic can supervise or perform an overhaul, and the expenses and difficulties encountered may be only great, not monumental. When it comes to overhauling truly antique powerplants—the little old radials and rotaries whose names hardly anyone even recognizes today—the problems multiply in inverse proportion to the familiarity of the engine type.

The owner will quickly realize, or be told, that the renovation of an antique powerplant can be as time-consuming as that of the rest of the airplane. The big problem, obviously, is parts; in some instances none may be available at all, or when they are available, they may be very difficult to track down. The obstacles are not insuperable, of course, because others have trodden these roads before and the devoted connoisseurs of antiques have a pretty good idea where to look for hard-to-get parts. The best luck one could have would be to live near someone else with the same engine, who has already overhauled it, and to be prepared to repay in whatever way is best the bushels of advice that will be asked for and given. Failing this, if no personal guidance whatever can be obtained, one simply has to dig up a copy of the engine manual and proceed, laboriously, alone.

A rebuilder who has no past experience with the insides of engines would not be well advised to cut his teeth on an antique, unless he happens to be a person of very definite, but untried, mechanical apti-

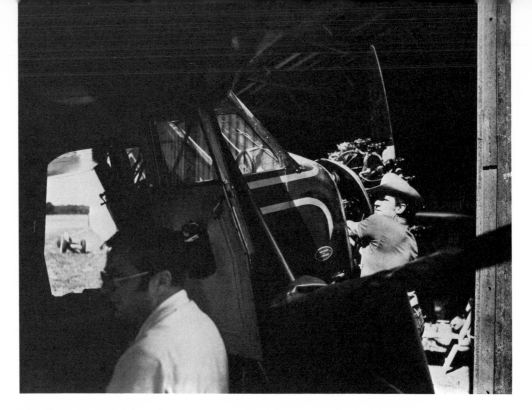

This Stinson got sick at a fly-in one year and had to be left behind by its owner, who wasn't able to get back to work on it until he came to the next fly-in a year later.

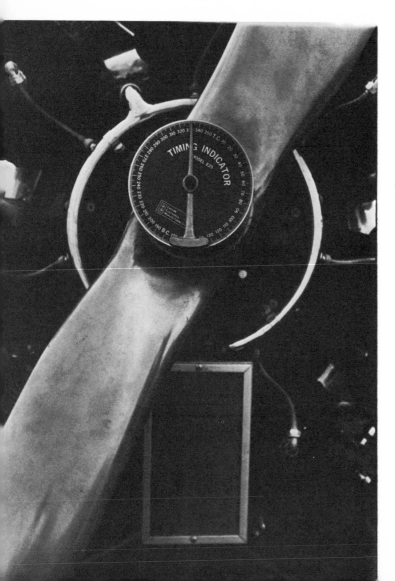

This timing indicator is a simple and effective device that should be in the tool complement of anyone working on their own engine.

tude. Although engine manuals make everything sound cut and dried, there is a great deal of finesse to be learned in practice, and much of it can be acquired working on any machinery at all, not just antique aircraft engines. No mistake is tolerable; one's woodwork or welding or doping may be a bit rough at first, but errors can later be corrected; with an engine, there is not so much latitude.

If the builder is mechanically inclined, however (and the mere fact that he is restoring an airplane suggests a certain ability), he may elect to rework the engine himself. At least he may elect to include doing so among his options—which also include buying a rebuilt engine from someone else, looking over someone else's shoulder while he rebuilds the engine, or shipping the thing off to a professional for a rebuild; or, for that matter, substituting a more modern engine in some sort of disguise (heresy, but done nevertheless).

There is much to be said for becoming intimate with one's own engine. For one thing, if you travel away from your home base and

Knowing your machine can mean the difference between moving on and getting stuck. Here Bill Rogers (right) and Richard Rausopher (left), both of Denton, Texas, repair the Kinner engine on Rogers's 1941 Ryan PT-22. The engine began to lose compression on one cylinder when the studs started backing out of a head.

trouble develops, you may be the only authority around. Furthermore, aggravation, delay, and expense can be avoided by a flyer who does his own maintenance on his own schedule. At the same time, he gains the confidence of knowing all his engine's strengths and weaknesses. For these reasons—and they are good, practical ones, to which most experienced flyers would subscribe—it is a good idea to do all or part of your own engine work if you are at all able.

One warning: it is not wise to begin an overhaul and then turn it over to someone else, unless that person is very familiar with the engine. Taking things apart is the way you get to know them; mechanics hate to have cardboard boxes full of parts dumped in front of them. Not that you can't do so in extremis—it just won't make you any more popular.

If you do the work yourself, consult a licensed mechanic in advance. Better still, consult several. You may be able to get recommendations from another antiquer on who is knowledgeable about your engine type. Some mechanics are more easygoing than others about signing off a nonmechanic's work, and you might as well find one who is happy to cooperate. Then discuss the whole procedure with him in advance, and try to get a clear idea of what he wants to see and what he may want to do himself. Much of the labor cost of an overhaul is in routine teardown and reassembly, which can at least be shared between a mechanic and the owner, but if you do your work in somebody else's shop or hangar, don't forget that to a mechanic his time is his livelihood, and if you pester him with questions and distract him from other work, he may as well charge you for the time and do your work himself. In other words, if you want to do the job yourself, do it yourself; but don't pretend to do it yourself while, in fact, leaning heavily on a professional all the time.

Apart from tools and lots of cleaning solvent, a good gadget to start off with is a Polaroid or other instant-print camera. Take pictures of your engine from every angle in good light, and make sure you have the focus right. It may not seem important initially, but months from now a single snapshot showing the way some bit of baffling was assembled may save you a great deal of grief.

After recording the assembled engine on film (assuming that you have bought an assembled engine, and not a lot of boxes full of parts), with the engine preferably in place on the airplane (installation details

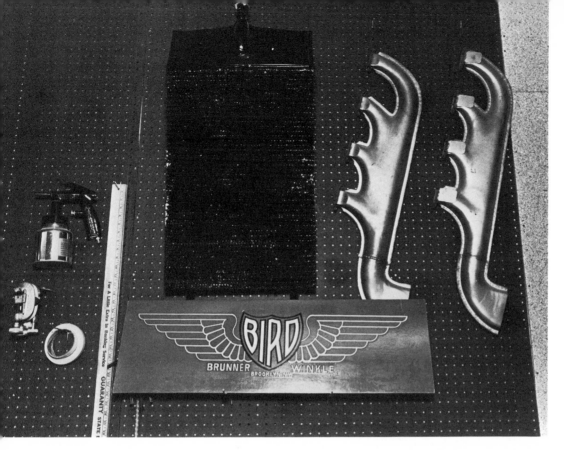

The radiator and exhaust manifolds for the OX-5 on Duane Golding's 1929 Brunner-Winkle Bird await reassembly.

are as important as the appearance of the engine itself), move the engine to a bench or an engine stand (the latter, which is preferable, may be welded up for a few dollars) and drain the oil, if there is oil in it. Keep it. You may filter it through a fine cloth to check it for metal particles or, if you prefer, send a sample (preferably the *first* oil to come out when you remove the sump plug) to one of several oil-analysis firms for spectroscopic analysis. This type of analysis is actually more useful to monitor the condition of an engine during its life than to determine the cause of death, but it can reveal areas of wear by telling you what type of metal particles are present in the oil and in what quantities. Since you are going to take the engine apart anyway, however, getting the oil analyzed is far from indispensable.

Then check the engine externally for damage, cracks, or indications of fuel or oil leakage. This will point to possible problem areas to which you should give particular attention during reassembly.

The engine should not be disassembled without the utmost care

This is the 220 Continental on Loel Crawford's 1941 Waco UPF-7. He bases it at Dacy Airport, in Harvard, Illinois, where Susan Dacy rebuilt her Stearman. What he learned in making the ignition harness ring for this engine helped Susan make one for her own Continental. Antiquers probably learn more about rebuilding their airplanes from each other than from anything in print.

and good organization. Parts should be stored in labeled boxes; each individual part should be labeled, if necessary. Orders of installation of bushings, washers, gaskets, and so on should be noted. Pistons, connecting rods, valves, bearings, rockers, and so on should all be numbered. All hardware should be catalogued, even if it is later to be replaced with hardware of modern manufacture.

Set aside the accessories—carburetor, magnetos, generator, and so on. They may be dealt with later or may be farmed out to specialty shops. You may need know-how to set up some accessories, such as carburetors; others, like certain types of magnetos, are quite straightforward.

All parts must be thoroughly cleaned. Different types of solvents or abrasives are used for this purpose, and an aircraft shop will tell you which should be used when. Cylinders, for instance, are typically glass-bead blasted. Crankcases are acid dipped and then treated with a corrosion-preventive process such as Alodine. After cleaning, all parts should be inspected for cracks, by magnaflux* in the case of ferrous parts, or by zyglo** or penetrant inspection for aluminum and magnesium parts; however, inspection for cracks should be preceded by a preliminary check, so that unsalvageable parts are not inspected.

There is bound to be wear on moving parts. Usually bushings can be replaced easily. Ball bearings and seals can generally be replaced out of modern stocks. Where possible, parts updates that do not detract from the authentic appearance of the engine should be made in the interests of future serviceability and replacement. Worn cylinders, pistons, rings, valves, and crankshafts present the most serious problems. It is not uncommon to have to have new pistons machined—a fairly costly process if you don't have one friend in the machining business and another with the engineering knowledge to specify alloys and design details (since machined pistons will differ in some respects from cast ones). Common problems are ring matching, groove design, and skirt length (to avoid collision with the crankshaft or master rod). As for the cylinders, the overhauler may choose between chrome plating followed by regrinding (to bring the bores back to a nominal size) or honing or boring out to a larger size. The choice depends on the pistons and rings; rings of suitable size and material must be found, and pistons with proper—not excessive—clearances. Ring gaps are particularly important in radials, where oil draining down into a bottom cylinder may produce "hydraulic lock" when the engine is turned over, thus bending rods or stretching the studs that hold the cylinders to the engine block. Chrome cylinder walls are very hard and resistant to wear and rusting; they may therefore be desirable for antiques that may be flown infrequently. On the other hand, chrome sometimes causes higher oil consumption than plain steel or nitrided barrels, and sometimes it flakes or peels from the cylinder walls. Plain steel walls are excellent in many respects, but they resist rust poorly and of course do not offer the option of returning to a nominal new-bore diameter.

Antique engines require the same inspection procedures as modern ones do; it is useful to have a modern overhaul manual for reference. (The manuals for Lycomings are much better and more complete

---

*An immersion process that reveals flaws in metals.
**A dye that will seep through and reveal minute cracks such as those that sometimes occur in cylinder heads.

The antiquer's version of "get out and get under." At least you don't always have to lie in the dirt.

than those for Continentals.) Valves, pushrods, camshafts, and so on must be checked for wear, corrosion, and runout; this is ideally a job for a professional shop with good measuring equipment. There is a lot of "feel" in the proper use of micrometers and indicators, which an amateur may not have.

A worn crank may be ground undersize, or it may be brought up to size by various means of adding metal to the journals. Remarkable repairs can be accomplished by a skilled welder, and by judicious application of the AC arc, added material can be made to look just like the parent casting. However, where highly stressed parts such as cranks, rods, and pistons are concerned, welding may be impossible because of the alloy or temper of the material.

After each part has been inspected, cleaned, and plated, anodized, or alodined, as the case may be, it should be stored in a dry dust-free environment or coated with preservative oil. Bare ferrous parts, in particular, should be stored in oil to prevent rusting. Prior to assembly, all parts must be cleaned with a general-purpose solvent, then air-dried and checked for contaminants. Bead blasting often leaves a seasoning of glass beads in the nooks and crannies of cylinders; care should be taken to remove these, as they are quite abrasive if they find their way into the engine oil.

Although automotive shops are frequently equipped to do much of the work you'll need done, it's wise to stick to aircraft shops, or at least to the better, more professional shops that cater to the auto-racing trade. The quality of work expected for autos is far below that required by aircraft, and even a well-meaning, careful shop may simply not have the habits and frame of mind necessary for turning out first-class work. Race cars require a concern for materials and processes similar to that neces-

This Curtiss Challenger engine on John Bowden's Robin has pistons that were custom-made by Jahn's in southern California. Jahns's primary business is to make pistons for hot rods, dragsters, and the like, but Bowden and S. K. Holmes, who did the rebuild, say that the custom pistons are probably better than those that originally came with the engine.

sary in aircraft work; but there is no match for a well-equipped, experienced aircraft shop for the big jobs like cylinders—especially if you can find your way to a shop that has worked on your type of engine before.

Engine assembly should be done in a dust-free environment and over as short a period as possible, to keep airborne dust from entering the crankcase in large quantities. The engine should be covered with a plastic dropcloth when it isn't being worked on. The supervising mechanic should be present or available for the assembly of the bottom end, which can normally be completed in a day. When pistons are placed in the cylinders, care should be taken to see that the proper ring gap is present and that ring gaps are staggered around the piston.

There are all sorts of exotic gasket-sealing materials on the market, some with very reputable names and unusual colors and textures, but the old standards like Titeseal are still as good as any. They have the indisputable merit of allowing easy disassembly; gaskets are rarely damaged and the sealing material can be easily cleaned up with volatile solvents like MEK.

When the engine is assembled and hung on the airplane, it should be carefully preoiled and greased. Old engines did not always have the provisions for pressure oiling, especially in the valve train on early radials, that later ones did, so the need for frequent and thorough greasing should not be underestimated. Adjustment of the valves is also tricky in the absence of hydraulic lifters, because the cylinders and the pushrods change length when they heat up and they don't usually change by the same amount. The first running is likely to reveal the need for some adjustment.

When the airplane has been securely tied down and carefully inspected by some competent person other than its doting owner, someone should be stationed alongside with a fire extinguisher (after a briefing on the smokiness of some old engines and of newly assembled engines generally) while the engine is turned over. Since this is usually done by hand, until everything has been tested the person at the prop should take the most pessimistic view possible of magneto grounding and of the willingness of the engine to start at the slightest provocation.

When the engine has been started, it should be run at a low-power setting (around 1,000 to 1,100 rpm) for two or three minutes and then should be shut down and inspected for fuel or oil leaks or for any other indication of things amiss. If there are none, then the time has come to fly.

There are two schools of thought on engine break-in, one holding that break-in should be accomplished by a long period of ground running, the other opting for immediate in-flight break-in at rather high-power settings. The weight of evidence is on the side of the latter, but that of sentiment stands with the former. Whichever method you and your advisors prefer, the break-in should be done with a noncompounded mineral oil, which should be changed after the first hour or so of running, to remove whatever dirt and fuzz have collected in the engine during assembly and so that you can check for metal particles, indicating serious wear or interference. Normally, mineral oil is used for the first twenty-five to fifty hours, and then a compounded ashless-dispersant (or "detergent") oil is substituted for the rest of the life of the engine. There are exceptions to these common practices, and peculiar engines, such as rotaries, may call for peculiar lubricants.

In theory at least, ring break-in should have been completed by the end of the first fifty hours, if not by the end of the first hour of high-power operation. Temperatures should be normal, and oil consumption should have stabilized at some acceptable level. High oil consumption, if it is not obviously due to a leak, may indicate improper ring/piston/cylinder fits—especially if spark plugs appear oily or caked on removal. Some early engines are simply oil drinkers by nature, however.

Incidentally, many old airplanes were not equipped with carburetor heat boxes, but they are a requirement today. Designing a carburetor heat box provides a real test of the ingenuity of the restorer. Airplanes that were certificated without them need not have them by law, but they are definitely worthwhile and contribute a lot to the safety of an airplane.

Although the overhaul of an unusual old engine may be difficult, actually keeping one running need not be. The older engines were robust and powerful and turned at low rpm, keeping wear and vibration low. They require more continuous care and attention than modern engines do, but they are not cantankerous just because they are old, and once properly set up, they can be kept running reliably for a long time.

11

The Airframe

FUSELAGE CONSTRUCTION

Although any material at all could be used for aircraft construction, and most have been, wood, metal, and fabric in various combinations were virtually the only ones used up to World War II.

The earliest airplanes had uncovered fuselage structures consisting of a truss of wooden poles (sometimes bamboo was used) diagonally braced with wire. This type of construction, called the Pratt truss, was supplanted by the somewhat simpler and more easily manufactured Warren truss, in which the wire diagonals were replaced by rigid members of the same material as the main longitudinal members (longerons). Corner attachments were made by gluing, nailing, or screwing metal or wooden plates called gussets to all the members of a cluster.

Several variants of the Warren truss were developed, including box structures, in which thin plywood sheets were glued over the truss, at first representing an outgrowth of the gusset idea but eventually

OPPOSITE
Dal Crites's Curtiss Pusher replica. Crites is one of the only pilots in the world who regularly flies this, one of the most primitive designs from the very earliest days of aviation. He has had extensive experience with the design, rebuilding it more than once after suffering some mishaps flying it. This specimen has an OX-5 engine. Crites built the Pusher partly by using notes taken while wielding a tape measure at the Curtiss Museum. The museum, located in Hammondsport, New York, contains an authentic Pusher that Crites once owned, crashed, rebuilt, and donated. After he made the donation, he started to miss flying the type, so he built himself this one.

The bamboo used in the aft portion of Crites's Pusher is visible here, as is the horse-blanket safety pin used to position the horizontal stabilizer.

This is a section of the Curtiss JN-4 Jenny—lots of wires and bolts with carefully formed woodwork, some of it routed. Many of the craftsmen who made the aircraft of this era learned their trade while fabricating horse-drawn carriages.

FUSELAGE SECTION - EARLY 1920'S

This section of fuselage shows the construction used in the early 1920's, as in the Sperry M-1 Messenger airplane. The fuselage was of veneer type and had 4 internal longerons and 1 false longeron at the bottom front section of the fuselage that extended back only to the end of the flooring. The longerons, square in section, tapered from 3/4 by 3/4 inch at the front to 1/2 by 1/2 inch at the rear. Fuselage covering was veneer and the bulkheads were plywood. All diagonal braces were solid spruce, but no diagonal brace wires were used. This type of construction was required to hold a load equivalent to a factor of 5.5.

A step up from the Jenny fuselage, this section of a Sperry M-1 Messenger used longerons instead of wires and had a veneer covering instead of fabric. Note the wooden plates, called gussets, in the corners.

An OX-5 engine mounted on Dale Crites's Curtiss Pusher replica. Although this engine works well for Crites, who purchased it from a fellow who happened by with one in the back of his pickup truck, it is not a popular powerplant with antiquers. Many were produced as part of the war effort during World War I, but they are not especially reliable and do not produce a lot of power for their weight. A few are found in the Jennys on the fly-in circuit.

replacing the diagonal braces altogether (many light aircraft are still built this way in Europe).

The plywood-skinned Warren truss, which was used in the popular de Havilland 60-G Gypsy Moth and DH-4, partially bridged the gap between truss and monocoque structures. *Monocoque*, a French word meaning "single shell," is a type of construction familiar in boats: the shape or skin of the vehicle, appropriately stiffened, itself serves as the main structural element. All modern metal aircraft are constructed in this form, or, more precisely, in semimonocoque, meaning that strong internal members are added to the monocoque shell to carry concentrated loads. Usually, these are limited to spars in wings and tail surfaces, and longerons in fuselages. (A distinction must be made between the spar or longeron type of member, which properly separates monocoque from semimonocoque construction, and the frame or stringer, which merely reinforces the monocoque shell and is more a part of the shell itself than a separate load-carrying member.)

Pure wood monocoque construction appeared very early, for instance in the beautiful oval fuselages of the German Pfalz fighters in World War I. Wooden laths were wound in a spiral around a mold and glued in order to produce this type of fuselage—a process that is rather hard for the restorer to duplicate today—or alternatively, plywood shells were formed, usually in halves, and then joined together over bulkheads. In addition to being difficult to build, wood monocoque structures needed a good deal of maintenance to prevent their warping and peeling apart. Much later, with the advent of more modern glues and protective coatings, wood monocoque construction was applied to such relatively advanced aircraft as the twin-engined British Mosquito fighter of World War II.

Unlike wood monocoque, the simple wooden Warren truss, skinned or not, is attractive to the modern restorer. The skills required by such simple woodwork are quite well known, and the necessary tools are to be found everywhere. Modern glues and paints remove many of the difficulties of wood construction and leave its advantages: lightness, rigidity, strength, immunity to fatigue.

Except for those that, like the Gypsy Moth, were skinned over the truss—the skin as the outer surface of the airplane—truss-framed aircraft were covered with a fabric fairing supported on a structure of stringers and frames that resembled, in detail, the strings and bridge of

The Lockheed Vega, one of the best-known early examples of a monocoque fuselage produced in quantity. The process by which the fuselage was first molded into two plywood half shells, then bonded together, is technologically quite demanding. That they were able successfully to resolve all the problems involved reflects great credit upon the Lockheed engineers. The process is described in detail in an excellent history of the Vegas by Richard Sanders Allen (see Bibliography). The Vega pictured here is part of the National Air and Space Museum, in Washington, D.C. It was used by Amelia Earhart to make the first solo flight from Hawaii to the U.S. mainland. Only two of these milestone aircraft are still flying.

a violin. On wings and tail surfaces the fabric supplied some torsional strength, as well as the aerodynamic surfaces necessary to produce lift. On the fuselage, the sole purpose of the fabric was to convert the homely square open trusswork into an aerodynamically smooth shape.

The wooden truss came gradually to be replaced by a similar structure of steel tubing with welded joints. Most early steel tube fuselages used 1023 steel. In the late twenties chromium-molybdenum steel, otherwise known as chromoly or 4130 (forty-one thirty), made its debut. Being strong, weldable, comparatively resistant to rust, and tough, so that it takes overstress by bending considerably before it breaks—obviously a desirable quality in an aircraft material—it has dominated steel tube fuselage construction ever since. It is also easily

The tough welded steel tubing fuselage of the Stearman. Not only was the construction of these fuselages rugged but the tubing was also filled with linseed oil, and these two things help contribute to the fact that there are a lot of Stearmans still around in good shape whereas other designs have long since disappeared.

Thoughtful design of anything means endurance. The Stearman's tailwheel suspension and steering controls are protected from the elements by a tough canvas boot, seen here from the inside.

and conveniently repaired by simple splicing techniques. The biplanes of the thirties, and monoplanes such as the Cub, generally used steel tube and fabric construction. The supporting interface between the truss and the cover was made variously of wood or metal, or combinations of the two.

In the thirties, the idea of metal semimonocoque structures began to take hold. At first, designers were skeptical of the thin-skinned metal shells, and inserted welded cages in the highly stressed areas around wing roots, landing gear, engine mounts, and cabin, particularly

The Spartan Executive represents a transition of sorts in aircraft construction. It is built somewhat as though its designers were hedging their bets, since even though its metal skin looks as though it were monocoque, it is actually supported by a framework of metal tubing. Up until this aircraft type was designed, the Spartan engineers had made only fabric-covered aircraft, which may account for the approach they decided upon. This beautiful example was the last of the thirty-four built, and it is owned by one of the most friendly and delightful antiquers in the movement, George Mennen, Jr. Like many Spartan owners, he used it frequently, including many trips to Florida from his home in Morristown, New Jersey. The Spartan has very docile flight characteristics and is an excellent cross-country machine. Yes, Mennen's company produces the aftershave.

Another nice feature of the Stearman from the standpoint of the restorer is that it has many access panels that make servicing the aircraft's various systems easier. This one opens up to expose the toe brake cylinder for the left gear.

The corrugated Duralumin skin of the Ford Trimotor close up. Control cable guides are mounted on the skin's exterior. One need not be an aeronautical engineer to imagine the drag produced by this type of construction. Still, the Fords were record setters in their time.

because the continuity requisite to monocoque construction was interrupted in those areas by windows, doors, and so on. The redundant and, it eventually developed, superfluous tubular cabin truss was included in monocoque aircraft even after World War II; its history stretches from the Beech 18 and Spartan Executive down to the relatively modern Mooney, Piper Apache/Aztec, and Meyers 200 designs. Finally it was eliminated, both because it entailed a weight penalty by making the cabin's metal skin nonworking, and because it represented a costly added complication in manufacture.

The Lockheed Vega is an interesting transitional design, first having been built with a wood monocoque fuselage (118 examples from 1927 on) and later with a Duralumin monocoque fuselage (10 examples, called DL-1s). A contemporary of Lindbergh's Ryan, the Vega, with its clean fuselage shape and cantilever wing, was a milestone of aviation history, serving a number of airlines and setting records in the hands of such people as Amelia Earhart and Wiley Post. The metal fuselages of Vegas were genuine monocoque structures, unlike those of the Spartan Executive (1936–40), which were only a "metallized" tubular truss. The Ford Trimotor introduced in 1926 was an all-metal design of corrugated Duralumin, a construction technique pioneered and patented by the German firm of Junkers; structurally sound, it was aerodynamically inefficient. It remained to the Boeing 247 and Douglas DC-2—introduced to airline service in the early thirties—to combine

All modern airliners are related to the DC-2, since its monocoque fuselage and multicellular wing construction provided the combination of strength and lightness that air transport designers have always needed. Only one airworthy DC-2 is left, owned by Colgate Darden, of South Carolina (there were 156 produced). His was manufactured in 1935.

aerodynamic finesse with monocoque construction in a pioneering design from whose basic principles airliner construction has never significantly deviated since.

FABRIC

Although fabric-covered airplanes are still being manufactured by several companies, fabric work is a disappearing art. There are only a few independent shops in the United States that would even attempt to take on a fabric job. They realize that it is time-consuming, laborious

Wayne Hayes dopes cotton tapes to the cotton blanket of his wing. The tapes go over the ribs and also over the seams in the blanket. A seam is seen here between two ribs, under the middle of the three tapes being secured. On the top of the rib at left may be seen the exposed cord from the rib-stitching job. Note that as an added refinement to keep everything looking nice, even though not required by the FAA, Hayes has drawn lines lengthwise on the fabric as guides for each rib stitch. It is this kind of tender care that justifies the oft-heard proclamation by an antiquer that "She's in better shape than when she left the factory."

work, and that to do a really good job would result in a bill for shop time that few customers would be willing to pay. There are exceptions to this—aircraft restoration specialists who work on old airplanes for a living and often do outstanding work—but, as a rule, today's shop has no interest in the cut-and-paste approach to aircraft construction.

This leaves the problem in the hands of the individual antiquer. Fortunately, there is enough information still available and there are antiquers around covering their own machines who can offer encouragement, advice, and guidance to the novice fabric worker.

This means that it is entirely possible for a person to do a covering job that is at least equal to, and frequently better than, one a professional might turn out, because a professional probably would not be able to devote as much time and patience to the task. In fact, as with many aspects of antique aircraft restoration, it is quite likely that the private individual who undertakes a fabric job himself can end up with results superior to those on the aircraft the day it left the factory.

Today's antiquer has advantages that his professional predecessor never had: a wider choice of fabrics—from the original cotton to the more durable synthetics; better quality, less flammable dope; and advanced tools, including spray guns, which make the job a lot easier than it was decades ago.

From a psychological standpoint, fabric work can be one of the most rewarding aspects of an antique restoration. It is certainly the most obvious manifestation of the restorer's skill. When his pride and joy is sitting out there on the flight line at a fly-in, a knowledgeable antiquer can take one look at the fabric job and tell you all about the kind of person who did the restoration.

A bad job will show up in uneven rib-stitching, poorly aligned tapes, dribs and drabs of dope, unevenness, blushing, orange peeling, and other flaws. In an outstanding job all the stitches will be spaced perfectly, tapes will be lined up with the ribs, there will be no dope deposits, and there will be nice, even paint.

But back to basics. There are essentially three kinds of fabric that can be used to cover an antique: cotton, linen, or one of the several types of synthetics. Each fabric has its own merits, and the reasons why an antiquer thinks a certain kind is the best soon become topics for endless discussion. However, most antiquers warn against mixing fabric types in the same aircraft—cotton tapes on synthetic cloth, for example, because the tapes will rot long before the synthetic, making a complete recovering job necessary.

Contrary to popular misconception, old airplanes were never covered with canvas. Most of them were originally covered with cotton similar to that used for dress shirts. In fact, Ruth Spencer, whose book *Aircraft Dope and Fabric* (see Bibliography) is essential reading before attempting a re-covering, once made herself some blouses out of material left over from an aircraft fabric job.

There are some good arguments for using cotton fabric on an antique. The purist who feels that a restoration is by definition an attempt to restore an aircraft to its original condition would say that if the aircraft was originally covered with cotton, it should again be covered with cotton. Another argument in favor of cotton is that it is by far the best material to use if one is interested in the smoothest finish possible—one where the weave of the fabric is hardly visible when the job is done. Such a finish can be achieved because the fibers of the cloth absorb the paint; with enough applications of paint and elbow grease (i.e., wet-sanding), the finish will be so smooth it will glisten in moonlight. Some antiquers feel this kind of eye appeal has a persuasive effect on the thought processes of the judges at antique aircraft competitions.

Marie Hayes wet-sands a wing of the family Waco. After a few hundred hours of wet-sanding, the edges of the tapes will be virtually invisible and an antiquer's enthusiasm for old airplanes may be completely gone. However, this is just one of the many restoration tasks that will test one's dedication level. Wayne and Marie Hayes have refinished every square inch of both the exterior and interior with hours of laborious rubbing just like this. The result is a rich luster.

THE AIRFRAME / 179

Also, some antiquers think grade-A cotton, the type of cotton used in aircraft fabric work, is easier to work with than either linen or synthetics. It is not as heavy as linen, nor as slick as the synthetics. Unsecured, synthetics have a tendency to slip off any surface—usually just as you are ready to stick them on with a little dope.

Although linen weighs more per square foot than cotton, it will last twice as long under the same conditions. Linen is more expensive than cotton, but the initial expense must be related to the amount of time you expect to leave the fabric on the airplane.*

There is a school of thought among antiquers which holds that a fabric job should not be undertaken with longevity as the prime consideration. This school feels that it is desirable to take the fabric completely off an antique every few years, have a look inside, and find out how well everything is holding up. These individuals would never use the long-lasting synthetics in their airplanes.

On the other hand, severe climate and poor air quality may make it desirable to use a synthetic fabric, since synthetics withstand a lot of punishment from the elements, even when the aircraft is tied down out of doors. Examples of synthetics are Ceconite, Sitts Polyfiber, and Razorback.

The general process of covering the aircraft entails fitting the fabric to the frame, then shrinking it to form a tight skin. There are two methods of covering the aircraft components: envelope, and blanket skins.

In the first method, an envelope is made by carefully unrolling lengths of fabric on top of a component such as a wing or fuselage. The fabric is then trimmed to leave a few inches of overlap, machine-sewn together carefully following the lines formed by the edges of the component, and turned inside out so that the end result looks like a giant fabric bag. It is then ready for the shrinking process. Ready-made envelopes can be bought for common aircraft such as Cubs and Champs.

In the blanket method, the fabric is once again carefully unrolled so that it lies perfectly flat on the surface to be covered. It is then trimmed to within about two inches of the framework to which it will be attached with lacquer cement or dope.

*Linen, which was used on many early aircraft, is virtually impossible to obtain today.

Lacquer cement is used to make the fabric adhere to wood, metal, or anything *except* another piece of fabric. Dope is used to join fabric to another piece of fabric.

There are two kinds of dope used by antique airplane addicts: nitrate dope and cellulose acetate butyrate dope. Originally, nitrate dope was the only kind available. Its biggest drawback is that the vapor is very explosive and burns rapidly. (Cellulose nitrate is better known as guncotton.) Old-timers always have a story to tell about the terrors of using nitrate dope.

Cellulose acetate butyrate, referred to as butyrate and pronounced "beauty rate," will burn, but much more slowly than nitrate and, unlike nitrate, it will not ignite from a static electricity or friction spark or cigarette ash. In the event of difficulties in flight, this could mean the difference between turning oneself into a super nova or making a successful forced landing.

After the basic fitting of the fabric to the aircraft component, the shrinking process begins. For the nonsynthetics, shrinking is accomplished with water; for synthetics, it is done with heat. In the past, every coat of dope would add to the amount of shrinking, and the process would go on for months after the fabric job was completed. Today, there are nontautening butyrate dopes available, and they are recommended by many antiquers.

Nonsynthetics are shrunk by rubbing, not wiping, distilled water into the fabric with a terrycloth towel or washcloth. The water is applied evenly so that the fabric tightens uniformly, since the shrinking is quite rapid.

Synthetics are tautened with either a hot iron or a professional-quality hair dryer.* Personal preference will determine which tool to use. The iron is rather unyielding; if left on one spot too long, it permanently glazes the synthetic. Hair dryers offer better control. You can be more selective about the amount of heat applied to any one spot, and you can also be much more selective about the area where you apply the heat.

Once the fabric has undergone its initial shrinking, the first coat of clear dope is brushed or sprayed onto the component. Before starting,

---

*Some aircraft supply outfits sell a device that looks exactly like a professional hair dryer but is made just for aircraft fabric work. It is much more rugged, being constructed primarily of metal instead of plastic. It is also more expensive, but worth the cost in the long run.

John Gokchoff dries dope with a "hair dryer" made for aircraft fabric work.

however, one must be certain that there has not been too much shrinkage, because it is possible to warp the aircraft's framework.

Since dope is used so extensively in fabric work, its prima donna temperament bears mentioning. Dope is easily affected by extremes of temperature and humidity. Any fabric work involving the application of dope must be done in an area where the temperature is at least 70° F— higher under conditions of high humidity. In addition, the work area should be well ventilated, but not drafty. Drafts can result in uneven drying; one spot will dry on the surface first instead of through the depth of the dope. This shows up as milky-white splotches and is called blushing. Retarder is especially important to add to your dope mixture to help keep it from drying unevenly on hot days with low humidity.

A Midwestern antiquer makes this recommendation: "When you shoot that first batch of dope and it blushes, you'd just as well quit right there and wait for the right day. You can use retarder and everything else, but when it still wants to blush, you'd just as well quit." (The right day, as mentioned, would be one with the temperature above 70° F, and preferably less than 50-percent humidity.)

The first coat of dope should be mixed with fungicide, to keep mold and mildew from growing on the underside of the fabric. One pound of fungicide is usually mixed with two gallons each of clear dope and dope thinner. In the case of Ceconite, some antiquers prefer to use nitrate dope and thinner instead of butyrate for the first coat, then switch to butyrate for all subsequent coats.

Next, tapes made of the same fabric as the envelope or blanket are cut to fit everywhere there is an edge on the component. This includes the ridges formed where the rib of the wing meets the fabric skin. Before fabric tapes are applied to these ridges, however, a special nylon-reinforced tape that looks like masking tape is laid along the outline of each rib. Cord is then used to sew the fabric onto the rib, a process called, logically enough, rib-stitching.

The fabric tapes are applied over the nylon-reinforced tape and stitching with dope brushed onto each side that is to adhere. When the tapes dry, two to six coats of clear dope are applied. Antiquers who have worked with both organic and synthetic fabrics point out that there is a big difference in how the dope adheres to each fabric. With cotton, the

John Gokchoff cuts fabric tapes for a PT-22 wing. The tapes will be applied to all the "edges" on the wing, including those formed by the ribs, as seen in this photo. In this re-covering job, the fabric forming the wing surface was not stitched with cord to the ribs but tacked on with a special reinforcing tape. The approved technique for applying this tape for rib-stitching and many other aspects of fabric work is described in the government publication *Aircraft Inspection and Repair*.

dope is absorbed into the fabric structure, making it adhere well; with synthetics, there is no absorption, so the fabric has to be trapped inside layers of dope.

At first, after the dope is applied, the damp fabric will hang limp and look rather pitiful; but after the first coat or two dries, the fabric will become taut. It is then that one feels an irresistible urge to tap one's finger on the fabric, just to hear it ping. No antiquer who has worked on aircraft fabric seems able to resist this temptation.

From this point, applications of silver dope begin. Silver dope is made by mixing either aluminum paste or powder with a half-gallon of dope thinner and adding it to three gallons of clear dope. Depending on whose advice you take, you can either apply two coats of silver dope, one after the other, or alternate each coat of silver with a coat of clear. In any event, each coat of dope should be sanded lightly and evenly for a smooth finish.

Additional coats of silver, up to about five coats, each wet-sanded, can be applied if you want an exceptionally high gloss. From two to twenty or more coats of colored paint are added last.*

It is easy to become carried away with the finishing process. Although it is possible to get enough dope on synthetics to fill in the weave, by so doing you probably will have used too much dope, making the aircraft needlessly heavy. Vintage planes need everything in their favor to enable them to perform reasonably well; weighing them down for the sake of looks is an injustice.

WOODWORK

Wood has many advantages for the home craftsman. It is a familiar material by which he will not be intimidated. Tools and techniques for working it are well known and readily available; equipment may be obtained at a wide range of prices (which is not true of some of the basic tools of metalwork, such as shears and brakes); advice is easy to obtain either from other woodworkers or from cabinetmakers and other such specialists.

Wood is also easily inspected and repaired, for the most part. Unlike metals, it does not fatigue: a wood part is either broken or it is

*The number of coats can depend to some extent on how thin you like the consistency of your dope.

sound. On the other hand, wood rots and deteriorates as metals do, but at least the deterioration is visible on the outside, whereas in metal it may be internal and hidden (such as inside tubing).

The convenience of wood is fortunate for the restorer of an antique, and many antiques are made of this material. Wood is simpler to work with than metal, so the antiquer can repair wood more easily himself.

Repair of the metal tubing that makes up fuselage trusses and the like almost always requires welding, so the restorer will probably farm the work out to a professional welder unless he happens to possess the skill himself.

The first step is obviously to find out what needs to be done, making written notes on what has to be replaced. (The to-be-replaced list usually gets longer and longer before it starts getting any shorter.) Take photographs; they may help in reassembly, and at the very least they might help some other builder.

Obviously, all inspection covers and access panels should be removed. You are looking for damage and/or deterioration. Damage may take an easily recognizable form, such as breakage, or it may hide in minutely cracked metal fittings or in separated glue joints, where it will be much more difficult to see. The importance of inspecting every nook and cranny may be judged from the condition of the airplane: if most of it is in a good state of preservation, it may not be necessary to burrow everywhere looking for hidden problems.

Deterioration may be less obvious at first. Usually it consists of moisture damage, either in the form of warping and grain-wise cracking, or of dry rot, which looks as though the wood were crumbling into sawdust. Moisture damage is most likely in places where water may have collected and stood, so bear in mind the position in which the airframe was stored. Accumulations of dirt at low points, for instance, probably have held moisture.

By sighting along covered surfaces and checking the alignment of parts with a level, you can get indications of joint failures or of warpage, as along the trailing edges of wings. Deformation often occurs where fabric is joined to the wooden frame, particularly at corners or at points where a load is concentrated or where several structural members are joined together.

Distortions in plywood-covered leading edges probably indicate rib damage or delamination. A decision must be made—on the basis of the general condition of the structure—as to whether a localized repair will be sufficient, or whether a complete disassembly is called for.

Plywood surfaces are often covered with a layer of fabric. If this fabric splits, or if the whole airplane is to be re-covered, the entire fabric covering is removed from the plywood, never only part of it.

Water penetration in thin wooden surfaces shows up as a dark discoloration or as gray stains running with the grain. If the discoloration is not merely superficial—that is, if scraping the surface doesn't uncover good wood underneath—then the wood must be replaced.

Since by law, glue joints must be stronger than the wood they bond, disassembly of glued structures usually damages one part or another. Try to confine the damage to the part you plan to discard anyway, but don't discard parts immediately after removing them; save them for future reference as templates. Sometimes they are a good guide for nail positions or alignment. Don't throw them away until you're sure you have your new part satisfactorily and permanently installed.

When you take off the fabric, this is what you could find. New varnish is needed, and any duplication of wood parts could require the application of several complicated reconstruction techniques, even in this one small section. This is an upper wing on a SE5.

In the case of damaged ribs, old ribs can be used to make templates for new ones. Having a sample before you makes your work much easier than does reading a set of plans.

FAA regulations state the repair procedures to be used. Approved techniques are not the only possible techniques, but by adhering to them you will be on a safe path and will have no trouble when it comes to relicensing your airplane. They are compiled in two publications, AC 43. 13-1A, *Aircraft Inspection and Repair*, and AC 43. 13-2A, *Aircraft Alterations,* which are available from the Government Printing Office for a few dollars. Much of what is found in books and articles on various aspects of airframe repair is actually lifted from these manuals. FAA representatives may be able to respond to inquiries about repair and restoration, but their answers may not be adequate; the government manuals have the final word.

Most of the wood used in aircraft construction is high-quality spruce, selected for its density, straightness of grain, uniformity, and sap content. Because it is screened and treated, aircraft spruce is more expensive than many woods; but it is an excellent material that resists warping, has a strength–weight ratio superior to that of mild steel (it has a tensile strength of 6,000 psi), and is tough and flexible.

The most highly stressed part of an airplane is often the wing spar—the main wing member carrying bending loads. The requirements of a spar are that it be as light as possible and that it resist the applied loads in vertical bending and (in the case of a biplane wing) in compression. Wire- or strut-braced wings have a much more uniform stress distribution than cantilevered ones. Since there is relatively little difference between the maximum and minimum stress levels, the spar can be of constant section throughout; and since a large part of the load is carried in pure compression or tension, it does not have to have the **I**-beam shape that is most efficient for cantilever structures. A spar of rectangular section resembling, for example, a one-by-four straight from the mill, is called a plain spar. This type is found on many biplanes, particularly as a rear spar carrying a smaller percentage of the loads than the front spar.

For weight saving, you can remove a lot of the wood in such a spar without affecting its performance significantly, since some parts of the rectangular section are much less highly loaded than others, and these can simply be dispensed with. One way of eliminating unnecessary material is by routing out portions of the spar on either side, leaving the

THE AIRFRAME / 187

A sample section of a routed spar, showing its resemblance to a steel I beam.

This Stearman wing has a routed spar. The gentle curve of the routing is visible under the numbers *18261* stamped on the spar. Several companies built Stearman wings, and they sometimes used routed spars, sometimes plain spars.

top and bottom intact, so that the spar begins to resemble a thick **I**-beam, sometimes with vertical fillers at each rib attachment.

Because routing is a comparatively time-consuming procedure, a similar effect may be more simply obtained by building a box spar with fore and aft webs of thin plywood and top and bottom caps of heavy material, usually tapered to match the strength requirements of the wing structure. A cantilever wing, for instance, has spar caps that are very thin at the tips and become very thick at the wing roots, where the bending stress is greatest. Biplane wings have different requirements, since each wing is supported at a number of points along the span.

Spars of the plain and routed type are comparatively easy to repair, since they are made of a single piece of wood. Box spars present the more difficult problems of multiple splices and holding the proper alignment throughout the repair. All are within the possibilities of a home shop, however.

Rib rebuilding is usually quite simple, though in an airplane like the Waco Taperwing, in which every rib is different from every other, it can be quite a chore. Generally, a sound rib is laid on a flat board and locating blocks are glued down to hold the raw material of the next wing in place during gluing. Once the basic template has been made, cutting and gluing the parts for more ribs is a quick and usually simple process. The airfoil sections of most older aircraft were not the products

Bows on the ends of airfoils are made in different ways. This one in the EAA Museum has been reinforced by wrapping it with tape.

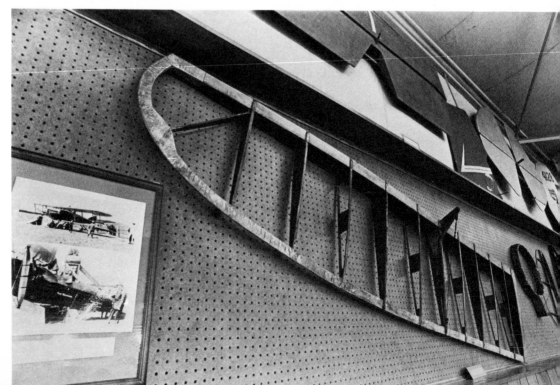

of much scientific study; designers just drew what they thought looked good, and that's what got built. In the twenties and thirties, sections developed in wind tunnels began to be widely used. For most restorations, therefore, it is more or less desirable to retain the airfoil contour with some accuracy when making new ribs, but the aerodynamic losses that might result from an inaccurate airfoil section are not likely to be noticeable. The irregularities in wing surface resulting from a mix of old and new rigs will be much worse.

Bolt holes in wooden wings are usually bushed with metal, or the wood is encased locally in metal reinforcing plates. Alternatively, major connections may be made entirely by metal fittings, which in turn are bolted to wooden subassemblies. In any case, if metal fittings show any sign of rust or wear, they should be removed, bead blasted, or otherwise stripped, repaired if necessary, and retreated either with a rust-resistant primer such as zinc chromate or Rustoleum, or with cadmium plate, or both. All metal parts that are cad-plated, by the way, should be baked to prevent their becoming brittle. If you have any plating done, take or send it to an aircraft shop that is familiar with the procedures used to prevent plating from changing the properties of the materials; a shop that specialized, for example, in decorative plating of car bumpers would probably not be acquainted with the problems associated with aircraft.

Because wood succumbs readily and irrevocably to a drill bit, you should use a good drill press for all holes that affect alignment or strength—which is to say, nearly all the holes in the wing. Hand accuracy, or even the accuracy of a cheap drill press, is not enough.

Whereas many antique airplanes have fuselage structures made of metal, most have wings made almost entirely of wood. The wing therefore represents the main challenge to the skill of the restorer, and he should perhaps put off attacking it until he has gained experience working on the relatively unimportant fuselage fairing structure. It would be a shame to make all the learner's mistakes on the most important part of the airplane.

Could be 1927, but it was 1977. Jack Greiner adjusts his goggles as Carl Buck, in the cockpit of this 1931 Waco QCF-2, and Alex Whitmore exchange a few words of wisdom.

12

First Flight

As the almost interminable process of restoration nears completion, you daydream more and more about the first flight. The thought of it is tempting and at the same time frightening. It is easy to imagine pitfalls, easy to imagine mistakes that would cancel all your efforts, easy to imagine that, somewhere, you have made some error, or some string of errors, that will turn and devour you as you take to the air. Ordinarily, when you first fly an antique airplane, you are not in the position of a person who has designed a homebuilt and now must test it; you at least know that your airplane once flew, that it is perfectly capable of flying, and that there is no reason why it should not fly again. Some restorations give little cause for anxiety; they are the conventional types, common, well known. Others are less ordinary.* If you want to make the first flight yourself—it is natural that you would—you may quite possibly be learning to fly the plane at the same time you are discovering that it flies. Much depends on the powerplant. A Continental is not likely to give many surprises; a Szekely might.

When the airplane is finished, an FAA representative must inspect and license it. He will be concerned about the same things you are—quality of workmanship, proper construction practices, safetying, and so on—the usual things that would concern any inspector, since he is unlikely to be intimately familiar with the particular type of airplane. He is, in fact, likely to be less of an expert on it than you, and his

*You may want to have someone familiar with the aircraft type do the test flying, as Susan Dacy chose to do (see Chapter 6).

signature on the certificate of airworthiness is a formality. Still, he may help you to see things that close association has hidden from you. Before he comes and after he has gone, you inspect and inspect again, checking every nut and bolt and curlicue of safety wire against the possibility that months earlier you left something just finger-tight and now have forgotten . . .

An old airplane wants to be tested on an old runway: grass, forgiving, caressing grass, not the concrete that grindeth and yieldeth not. If no grass field is to be found, a hard-surfaced runway will do, but the extent of damage if you drag a wing in a ground loop (heaven forfend—but it is possible) may be greater. The fact that a grass field is not as smooth as a hard-surfaced one is unimportant; old airplanes were made to land and take off in farmers' fields, and a few gopher mounds and chuckholes mean nothing to their big wheels and rugged gear. Lumps and holes are not likely to be encountered on most grass strips, however. Because of the small tires of modern tricycle-gear airplanes, grass runways are usually kept in good repair.

Unless you have been working on your airplane at the airport, you'll have to truck it there, which will mean assembling it at the airport before flight. Ideally, a weekend should be devoted to the event, so that there is ample time for everything. You truck the plane to the airport on Saturday morning; you have lunch. You assemble it in the early afternoon. You inspect it thoroughly, and then have time for some preliminary tests before evening.

Few pilots take the trouble to test everything exhaustively after assembly and, for the most part, no harm comes of it. Ideally, the engine should be run in an extreme nose-down attitude and an extreme nose-up attitude to verify that there is adequate fuel flow; but if the fuel system has been reassembled as it was on the original airplane, and if, as is usually the case, it is a gravity-feed system, that test can be omitted.

The controls should all be tested on the ground for tightness and correctness of stick and control-surface movement—people have paid the ultimate penalty for the minor sin of rigging ailerons backward—and it should be verified by test and inspection that no controls can possibly lock over center in any part of their travel. Rigging checks should no longer be necessary, but rigging and control travel should be checked with an angle level and recorded.

The needs of the engine during the first flight conflict with those of the airframe. If the engine is freshly overhauled, it should be run a little on the ground and then run for a while at normal power in the air; but the first step in test flying the airplane—a series of short hops down the runway—conflicts with this sequence. The compromise must favor the airframe, as a matter of safety.

But the engine should not be forgotten. You run it for a few minutes on the ground at a power setting somewhat above idle, having checked, if it's a radial, for hydraulic lock in the lower cylinders by turning the engine over several times carefully by hand.* Sitting in the cockpit with the engine idling, you experience for the first time the airplane you have restored. It is a living thing, shaking and murmuring as the prop blades blur and the engine coughs its irregular tattoo. You are chocked and tied, but you begin to sense what it will be like to trundle down the runway and float into the air.

After a few minutes of running, you shut down the engine and inspect it. You've left the cowling off and have had a friend standing by with a fire extinguisher, but there has been no fire, and now you crouch under the engine, looking for the dribbles and stains of escaping oil. The cooling metal creaks. Old engines, especially radials, leak oil; it's a fact of life and has nothing to do with the quality of an overhaul or the condition of an engine (not necessarily, at least). But you're looking for something abnormal or excessive. If there's nothing, you move on to stage two.

Again, you check everything; walk around; look from a little distance to make sure the angles are all right. Secure the cowling. Take your time. Some people say it's best to keep first flights a secret, so that dozens of friends don't show up and produce, even unwittingly, an atmosphere of urgency. But it's hard not to have everyone there, so you just have to make it clear that first flights proceed at a very deliberate pace.

Now you're ready for taxiing tests—or practice, if you like. Someone props the engine (more than likely) and you sit there in the cockpit, tentatively moving the throttle back and forth, feeling the engine pick up and settle down again as the airplane rocks on its gear with the changing torque. You exchange a few words with a companion through the shuffling of the propeller and the hiss of the wind, and then you are

*Hydraulic lock in a radial can be overcome by removing the plugs and draining the excess oil that has accumulated in the cylinders.

ready. The chocks are pulled away, and you test the brakes. The airplane rolls forward a few inches, you brake; a few inches more, and you brake again. Then you let it roll, gently nudging the throttle. It's apparent immediately that you have to do with a creature that already knows its tricks. The pedals bring the tail around smartly. The gear jounces over the grass with perfect assurance. It is not the airplane that needs practice, you begin to realize; it's you. You cut the throttle and pull the brake handle, and the airplane bounces to a stop; you gun it again, and it rolls forward, then arcs widely around as you press the rudder bar. You soon see that the airplane is not so delicate as your years of nursing it have led you to believe; it's a rugged thing, and now at last it's in its element.

These preliminaries are bound to take nearly all day. Perhaps on the following day, you're ready to make a few high-speed runs on the runway. You announce your intention: accelerate, lift the tail, chop the throttle, roll out without braking. Cameras are at the ready.

The airplane responds with a surprising surge of power to its big, slow-turning propeller; the tail comes up quickly, and, as quickly, you reduce the power and let the plane coast to a stop, the tail settling slowly and then hitting the grass with a jolt. You've used only a third of the runway; you do it again, then taxi back. Now taxiing has become second nature; you're doing it with aplomb, and your uncertainty and anxiety have largely been shifted over to runway handling. This too, after a few runs along the runway, seems simple, until you get too cocky and a little careless and as you're slowing down, suddenly the airplane gets itself sideways and does a slow, half-hearted ground loop. People come running up, but there's no damage. It's just the airplane's way of warning you not to lose your respect for it. You make a couple of taxi runs again, working the rudder pedals harder and looking for a sense of their power and response.

The sun is low, but there's still time for one more step: a short step into the air. You've been going nearly fast enough—just a couple of miles an hour more and a little back pressure, and you'll lift into the air.

Again you announce your intention; again the cameras. You accelerate; the tail is up. The antique airspeed indicator is wiggling, but you

OPPOSITE
John Bowden takes off from his hilltop "runway."

can't trust it too much; things feel about right, and you ease the stick back a little. At first, nothing, and then, suddenly, the bouncing stops and a strange smooth sashaying motion takes its place, and the ground shifts downward a little. You're in the air. The puttering roar of the engine, the wind ruffle and noise; the end of the runway seems suddenly too near; you cut the throttle, the airplane parachutes back to the ground, all too quickly for you to catch it, there's a creak and a bounce and the tail hops up and down, and then finally you catch up with things and steer the airplane authoritatively as it slows down. Half the runway is still ahead of you as you turn off to taxi back.

You may as well stop for the day; you won't find a better feeling than this to stop on. Your baby has had her baptism of air, and she's taken it well. Tomorrow, to the sky!

You'll begin the next day's activities by reviewing today's, examining the airframe closely, uncowling the engine and inspecting for leaks, checking the fuel, verifying all the cable tensions and the securities and safetyings of nuts and bolts. In your mind you'll review what you know of the characteristics of the airplane. Perhaps you've already flown others of the type; in that case, there's no problem. Perhaps you've only heard about the airplane's quirks—the sudden loss of rudder power as the tail comes down on landing, or the adverse yaw at high speeds, or the sudden steepness of the glide angle as power is reduced—and have yet to learn how they really feel. The reputations of some old airplanes are full of exaggerations; other planes have oddities to which hangar flying cannot do justice.

The routine of start-up is already beginning to seem familiar. You'll taxi out and, perhaps, wait for a departing Cherokee to clear the runway. You'll have a better sense by now of the length of the runway and of what you can expect to do in it. You'll ease in the throttle, bump along, lift the tail, lift off, tentatively make small movements of the controls and see how the airplane feels, then settle down and taxi slowly back. You'll repeat this ritual several times, and then you'll be ready for a flight.

Again at the start of the runway, you'll settle into your seat, tighten your safety belt for the umpteenth time, review the instruments, and try to still the beating of your heart. You feel, on the one hand, like stopping time here, but on the other, like hurrying its passage. Everything is all right. You'll push the throttle forward smartly, with determi-

nation that this is the moment of truth; the familiar bouncing accelera-
tion, the tail coming up, the liftoff—but this time with no thought of
throttling back and setting down again on the grass. The throttle stays
open and you lift away, acutely aware of the pocketa-pocketa of the
engine, the wiggling of the needles on the dials before you, the life that
now feeds back through the stick into your hands, the tension in your
ankles as you try to stop pressing both feet hard against the rudder bar.
The trees fall away and slide by below. You bank a little, feeling with
nervous acuteness the little jounces and thumps of thermals and eddies
in the air. The runway comes out from behind you on the left, smaller
now; the gauges are normal—airspeed, oil temp, fuel pressure, rpm—
and the airplane seems confident and impassive. It's hard to keep the
airspeed steady, but the altimeter records your ascent with little upward
jerks. The vibrations, at first alarmingly numerous, now begin to fall
into a monotonous pattern and to seem almost reassuring. You will
spiral up above the field, staying within gliding distance, watching the
engine temperature, getting the feeling of the controls, from time to
time forcibly clearing the tension from your legs and shoulders, trying
to keep up with the strange mixture of anxiety and elation that fills you,
trying to remind yourself that this is only the first of hundreds of hours,
not the last.

When you are a couple of thousand feet up, if you're like most
people, you'll start to think about getting down. Not that you're not
enjoying the airplane; it's rather that duty seems to require you to keep
a businesslike head, keep on testing and not tempt fate. You are here,
you'll tell yourself, to try out taking off, flying, landing; landing still lies
ahead.

When you lower the nose, you'll be rattled at first by the increasing
sound as the airplane picks up steam, the engine turns faster, the
vibrations change. You'll throttle back. Your hand on the controls will
get lighter; you'll open your ears to the sounds of the wind in the wires
and the subtle details of the puffs of exhaust and the muffled thudding
of the turning prop. You'll look over the side and see the little knot of
people down below, the far horizon, the immense sky, another airplane
on the downwind leg. The paradoxical impatience to land will assail
you again and you'll throttle back, listen to the new sounds, feel the
airplane begin to settle, watch the instruments. Established on the way
back down, you feel an almost reckless sense of confidence and com-

mand; you rock the wings steeply from side to side, maneuvering with a fresh *élan* and exercising the throttle with growing authority.

If you're a pilot with plenty of experience in antiques and flying this particular aircraft type is second nature to you, the approach should present no problem. If not, you'll be feeling your way through a maze of unfamiliar sensations. You'll fly a generous standard pattern, not too high, keeping your eye on the touchdown point and keeping the airspeed at a steady value while adjusting the rate of descent with the throttle. The trick will be to get into landing position right at the beginning of the runway, so that you can have time to take care of any uncertainty about whether or not you are landing at the correct speed. First time around you'll probably want to make a wheel landing; but you don't want to come in with too much speed, because if you get to bouncing or porpoising you could be in trouble. You'll get right down above the grass and let the speed bleed off. You'll be alert for the first feeling of contact and ready to push the stick slightly but smartly forward, not enough to pitch the nose down much, but just enough to keep the tail from dropping and the airplane from jumping back into the air. The trick of a good wheel landing is to maintain the level attitude, tail up, keeping pressure on the main gear until the tail settles of its own accord for lack of enough wind to hold it up. Then you'll be going slowly enough to handle the rollout with the tailwheel alone.

You'll be grateful, as the wheels touch, for the feeling that you've been there before, yesterday and today, at this point between the air and the ground where the forces that dominate the airplane begin to work through the wheels rather than the wings. If you can touch at the right speed, going in the right direction, half the battle is won. If you don't, you may get squirrely on the runway, battling in a sudden panicky moment the bewildering loss of synchronization between your control inputs and the behavior of the plane. But with luck, in a few seconds, things will have settled down and you'll be taxiing back, feeling like a heap of gelatin.

A pilot's first flight in an unfamiliar airplane, especially an *old* unfamiliar airplane, is like a meeting of two strangers uncertain of each other's intentions. On rare occasions, it turns out very badly. Most of the time, it is the beginning of a friendship. It is the beginning of true understanding of why you went to all the trouble in the first place; why you restored an antique rather than buying a factory-fresh airplane. As AAA President Bob Taylor puts it: "To fly the aircraft is the ultimate experience, but the care and love that keep an antique flying are important as well. When a pilot knows intimately the wood, the glue, the smell of dope and nuts and bolts that make up his airplane, then he too is a part of that flying machine, and each flight will be an *experience* and not just a passage from A to B."

That the flight is an experience, and not just a passage, is perhaps more true of the first flight than of any other.

You can get plenty of free advice when you have a problem at a fly-in, and some of it may even be helpful.

13

Fly-in

It is like the Olympics, the America's Cup, the Kentucky Derby. It is the most important event of its kind, the World Series of antique aircraft. To the antiquer, it is a living affirmation every year that the thousands of hours he has spent in solitude laboring on his craft have been for a good purpose. The event is called a fly-in, which is the most literal of descriptions. Arrive early enough and you can watch them fly in, wonderful artifacts entering the traffic pattern both from out of the past and right smack in the present. One can watch them as they settle onto the runway, gleaming points of pride.

At a fly-in, an antiquer faces the critics—friendly and otherwise. If his job has been done right, friendliness reigns. What has gone into his restoration is appreciated roundly by others who have been through it all themselves—the searching for parts, the many errors, with all their trials, and the long chain of frustrations.

Of all the fly-ins in the United States—no, in the *world*—Blakesburg is the most important. It is the biggest; it carries the most prestige. It is held at Headquarters.

A stone's throw from the tiny Iowa farm town from which the world's greatest fly-in derives its name lies the nerve center of the Antique Airplane Association. To this spot come the antiquers to replenish their energy and to demonstrate their skills.

There is a perceptible effort each year at Blakesburg to make old airplanes and their pilots feel at home. The grass runways will incorrigibly never be paved. The cornfields that surround Antique Airfield will remain unthreatened by the creeping concrete of suburbia.

In this relaxed, informal environment the restorer shows off his airplane. He meets in person, at last, the friends with whom he has discussed by mail or phone the fine points of bringing an airplane to life. He obtains new ideas for working on his craft. Communal discourse is S.O.P.

Given this, it is easy to see why Blakesburg is an important point of reference each year to any dedicated restorer of antique flying machines.

In pictures and a few more words, here is Blakesburg, along with other major fly-ins.

Alex and Marti Whitmore in their Travel Air L-4000 near Parsons, Kansas.

Two fly-in regulars do a formation takeoff at Tri-City Airport near Parsons, Kansas. R. J. Hardin (above) in his rare 1935 Waco YOC, George Hefflinger (below) in his 1939 Waco YKS-7.

Alex and Marti Whitmore taxi their Travel Air L-4000 at Tri-City Airport, Parsons, Kansas.

The 1943 V-77 Stinson of Calvin Bass of Tulsa, Oklahoma, arrives at the Atchison, Kansas, fly-in. This big, graceful antique has a wingspan of some 42 feet, which has forced more than one owner to search for quite a while before finding a tee hangar big enough. The V-77 was the military version of the Stinson SR-10 Reliant, manufactured by Vultee after it bought Stinson. Vultee built five hundred, most of which were sent to Britain's Royal Navy during World War II. After the war, 350 were repatriated and sold as surplus, several of which are still flying. In spite of their unspectacular performance statistics, they are spacious and comfortable cross-country machines, which may account for their popularity. Another reason may be the unique lines, which have given the plane the nickname Gullwing. It is one of the few antiques that is as pretty on the ground as in the air.

The 1940 Buecker Jungmeister of John Hickman, from Beeville, Texas, comes in over the corn at Antique Airfield, Blakesburg, Iowa.

Blakesburg is located in Iowa's corn belt, so naturally there is a "corn boil" during the big fly-in. And, of course, if you are going to have corn on the cob, you need to have a can of beer to go with it . . .

When things get too crowded inside Elaine's, you just go across the street and get a picnic table. That's Howard owner John Turgyan in the right foreground.

BELOW

This is the "Miss Blakesburg" contest, a riotous parody of all the vacuous pretentiousness of a beauty contest. The winner is selected on the basis of audience choice—who gets the most applause—not by a group of celebrity names who couldn't care less and would rather not be there in the first place except for the substantial fee involved. The audience knows the contestants personally, and the contestants know the audience. (In this case, one of the contestants is being questioned about the possibility that she is "in a family way.")

Just like the autos of yesterday, yesterday's airplanes require that their owners frequently "get out and get under," as it said in the song. This man doesn't *have* to grovel around on the ground like this. Claude Gray makes enough money as a DC-10 pilot both to pay his mortgage and pay someone else to do the groveling. But here he is—and a nicer person you'd never want to meet. Not an iota of braggadocio about the way he restored this 1927 American Eagle, one of the rarest flying machines on the antique circuit and one that has one of the most cantankerous engines ever mounted on airplanes, the 90-hp OX-5. It's not the first antique he has restored, and probably won't be the last, either. (This American Eagle is the only 1927 model still flying. Other airworthy Eagles are usually 1928 or 1929 models. Gray co-owns the Eagle with a partner, Bob Groff.)

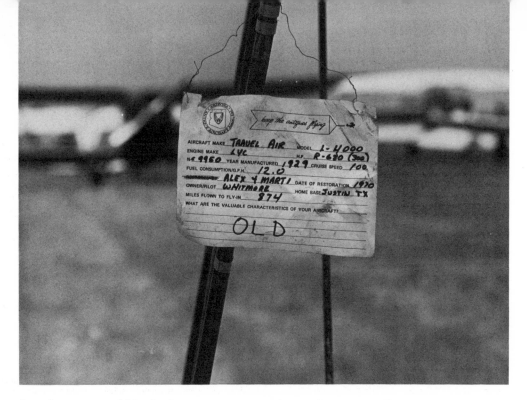

An information card like this hanging on your airplane is de rigueur at fly-ins.

Alex Whitmore takes off in tight formation with George Hefflinger in his Waco. The scene is at Tri-City Airport, Parsons, Kansas. Whitmore's aircraft is a 1929 Travel Air L-4000.

The farmers of Blakesburg think that the big fly-in is a great idea. They don't seem to mind at all having a lot of old airplanes flying over their houses. Perhaps there is some kind of a kinship between rugged individualists that generates this positive attitude. Note that there are no glasses on Elaine's bar.

The main intersection of downtown Blakesburg at midday.

"Doc" Lindquist holds the morning pilots' briefing during the August 1975 fly-in at Blakesburg.

This is the "meteorological office" at Blakesburg, the source of a lot of head shaking during the 1977 fly-in, which may become known as the year of the monsoon. Fly-in organizers will arrange with the Federal Aviation Administration to set up a temporary facility like this if the fly-in is big enough, as Blakesburg certainly is. The FAA, which is extremely cooperative and helpful when it comes to something like this, assigns a full-time staffer to man the facility and set up its special equipment, such as a weather information teletype and a facsimile weather map transmitter. In this way, all the latest meteorological information is available to fly-in pilots, just as at any permanent Flight Service station manned by the FAA at an airport.

Getting the oil moving in the 300-hp Lycoming engine of Alex Whitmore's Travel Air 4000. Alex's wife, Marti, is on the right.

Pat LaForge and his brother Greg make *ohs* and *ahs* as future antiquers. They're checking the cockpit layout of Dick Geist's Davis V-3 at Tri-City Airport near Parsons, Kansas. Both young men hail from Parsons.

Dave Warren serves two kinds of coffee at his coffee tent . . . Dave's tent is an institution at the Blakesburg fly-in. Many antiquers have their own cups with their name and the Antique Airplane Association logo on them. Dave is a mechanic for American Airlines. The profits from his beverage enterprise go to support the Airpower Museum, situated next to the headquarters of the Antique Airplane Association.

Ms. Barbara Desenberg conducts the Blakesburg High School band in a serenade to the antiquers.

IV

COLLECTIONS

This Grumman G-22 is one of a series of different aircraft types sponsored for air-show work by Gulf Oil. Each one was called *Gulfhawk*, and this one is *Gulfhawk II*. In the hands of Al Williams, it presented spectators with some of the most thrilling aerobatics ever seen. Only one other person flew it, Ernst Udet, the famous World War I ace. In addition to the air-show routines, Gulf used the aircraft for testing its products under extreme operating conditions. The machine is part of the Smithsonian's National Air and Space Museum.

Collections of antique aircraft come in all sizes, up to more than 100 machines. In a sense, even an individual antiquer with only one old airplane has a collection—a collection of one. Practically every antique represents a unity of parts—old, new, and remanufactured—that have been gathered from all around the country. So the individual antiquer with one old airplane has much in common with the collector who may have a dozen planes or the museum curator who has a hundred. Each of them has scoured the land for the machinery he wanted, then scoured it once again after finding the machinery, to locate missing parts.

Since all collectors have so much in common in their antiquing experiences, interests, and inclinations, it takes but a split second for two or more of them to get involved in conversation. The amount of information that can be shared, exchanged, and recalled in a matter of minutes is amazing. Historical facts are recounted; restoration techniques are reviewed; and stories of triumph and tragedy are told again and again.

All of this is inspired by inspecting and sometimes even flying the machines in a collection. Correspondence between collectors—of whatever numbers—is helpful, but there is no substitute for a visit in person. There are many collections around the country that contain aircraft of particular interest to antiquers. Some of them are of interest because of their historical significance; others are either duplicates or related to types already restored—machines that are part of the active antique movement.

In some cases, a collection offers a chance not only to observe and compare static displays of finished and partially finished aircraft, but to see restoration work on static displays actually taking place and to talk with those undertaking the task of rebuilding an old plane. Several collections, such as those at the EAA and the Smithsonian, have their own restoration shops, and antiquers are welcome when visiting arrangements are made in advance.

So a visit to a collection can be a highly profitable experience for an antiquer, and a chat with the person responsible for the collection usually demonstrates that he is as fascinating as his artifacts.

Here are some of the most interesting collections.*

*Some of the following material has been taken (with permission) from an excellent guidebook entitled *Aircraft Museum Directory*, which may be obtained from Quadrant Press, 19 West 44th Street, New York, New York 10036.

This Buecker Jungmeister is a "collection of one." This one belongs to John Hickman, of Beeville, Texas. The Jungmeister is a favorite of antiquers who like aerobatics. Buecker was a German navy pilot in World War I. He moved to Sweden after the war and got involved in aircraft manufacture. He returned to Germany in 1932 and brought a talented Swedish engineer named Lars Andersson with him. Their first effort was the 105-hp Jungmann, which was a nice aerobatic biplane but nothing exceptional. Their second effort was a refinement of the Jungmann, which they called the Jungmeister. It had a 160-hp Siemens Halske radial, like Hickman's. The type is a fine aerobatic machine. Hickman's is one of several produced in Switzerland under license and one of a handful that were purchased and imported into the United States. Hickman's is marked U-79. Its sister ship, U-80, is owned by Phil Dacy.

A 1917 Curtiss JN-4D at the EAA Museum. Hundreds of bits and pieces of wood have to be replaced and duplicated, including, in this case, some in oak, not just spruce.

The shop of the Experimental Aircraft Association always has at least a dozen projects under way, such as the Waco in the background and the Travel Air in the foreground.

This Pusher hangs in the terminal of the Tulsa Airport. It was flown by Billy Parker, pilot for Phillips Petroleum.

Aileron detail on Parker's Pusher. Note the skid on the tip of the lower wing. Since only clear dope has been used on the fabric, the outline of the rib-stitching and the tapes can be clearly seen.

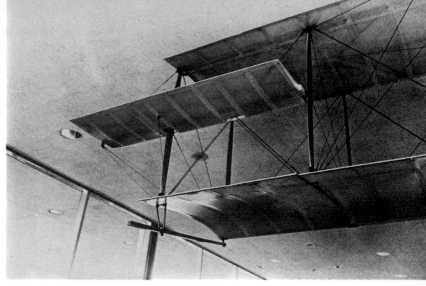

Detail of the empennage of Parker's Pusher.

There is an interesting trend around the country toward putting old aircraft on display in airline terminals. This replica of the *Spirit of St. Louis*, a modified Ryan B. 1, was one of three built for the Hollywood film about Lindbergh. The genuine article is on display at the National Air and Space Museum in Washington, D.C.

The 1935 DeHavilland 85 Dragon.

The 1929 Ford 5-AT-B Trimotor. The horseless carriage on the left is part of a car collection.

The Lincoln Page LP-J. Of the 150 examples manufactured between 1927 and 1928 by the Lincoln Aircraft Company, in Lincoln, Nebraska, this is the sole airworthy example.

The 1935 Stearman-Hammon Y-1S, which has a 150-hp Menasco engine.

CALIFORNIA · Morgan Hill · Hill Country

The collection at Hill Country is certain to interest the antiquer. It contains over two dozen aircraft, most of which are lightplanes of the sort that make up the active and airworthy segment of the antique movement. Irv Perch, owner of the collection, says that practically all the aircraft are in flyable condition and that many are flown during a special October event. Included are some very rare and unusual examples of interest, such as a Stearman-Hammond Y-1S. This radical departure from contemporary lightplane design was the winner of a controversial contest held by the Bureau of Air Commerce in an effort to inspire the creation of inexpensive machines that would be exceptionally safe to fly. Not incidentally, the collection also includes an airworthy Ford Trimotor.

Aircraft of interest to antiquers:

1927/28 Lincoln Page LP-J
   (sole airworthy example)
1929 Ford 5-AT-B Trimotor
   (one of the last three flying)
1930 New Standard D-25
   (sole airworthy example)

1935 DeHavilland 85 Dragon
   (once owned by British
   Railways!)
1938 Luscombe 4
   (sole airworthy example)

CALIFORNIA · San Diego · San Diego Aero-Space Museum

The entire stock of fifty airplanes in this museum was destroyed in a tragic fire on February 22, 1978. The only item to survive was a piece of moon rock in a fireproof safe. Four airplanes that were stored elsewhere form the nucleus of the current attempt to rebuild the museum.

CALIFORNIA · Santa Ana · Movieland of the Air

Few people make part of their living restoring and flying old airplanes. Among those who have are the late Frank Tallman and his colleagues at Tallmantz (Tallman-Mantz) Aviation, which is where Hollywood goes when it needs to create footage that includes old airplanes.

Like other museums where some of the exhibits still earn their keep in the skies, Movieland of the Air is partially a hangar for the active Tallmantz Aviation properties and partially an inactive collection of airplanes, parts of airplanes, and sets used in films.

The collection of aircraft changes all the time, according to the needs of the business—World War I replica fighters, barnstorming Jenny types, the L-1 Stinson, and so on. There is plenty here to absorb an antiquer's attention for hours.

Almost forty aircraft.
Aircraft of interest to antiquers:

Jenny used in *The Great Waldo Pepper*	Blériot XI replica 1934 Ryan ST

DISTRICT OF COLUMBIA · Washington · National Air and Space Museum

The new National Air and Space Museum was established by the Smithsonian Institution. Placed on a three-block tract on Washington's Capitol Mall, the museum consists of four marble cubes separated by three enormous glass bays. Visitors enter by the middle bay. There, hung in the epicenter of this breathtaking eighty-foot-high greenhouse, is the original Wright *Flyer*. In

In 1924, the U.S. Army sponsored the first successful round-the-world-flight attempt. It dispatched four Douglas World Cruisers from Seattle. Two completed the flight—in a little over fifteen days. This one, named *Chicago*, is now in the National Air and Space Museum.

This racer was used in 1939 by that colorful flyer Roscoe Turner, to win his last race before retiring. Turner took the Thompson Trophy for an unprecedented third time. To win, he had to lap the entire field after having cut a pylon. Turner drew up the basic design himself and called it the RT-14 Meteor. As was his wish, it has become part of the Smithsonian collection.

one corner hangs what may be the world's most famous airplane, Charles A. Lindbergh's *Spirit of St. Louis.*

The museum contains twenty-three separate display areas. As you enter, you'll want to head in all directions at once.

To the left and below a small balcony, poised in space beneath glass and a spider web of steel tubing, is a silvery Douglas DC-3, its gear retracted, suspended motionless in its last flight. This particular room is a celebration of the age of commercial aviation. Slowly one becomes aware of, first, a Pitcairn Mailwing, then a Ford Trimotor, then a Boeing 247. Off the left wing of the DC-3 is a Northrop Alpha, reflecting in its polished skin countless loving hours of restoration by employees of Trans World Airlines.

In the World War I gallery, a Spad VII can be seen hanging inverted as if doing a victory roll above a Fokker VIII.

There are several historically noteworthy airplanes in addition to the *Flyer* and *Spirit of St. Louis.* One can see Otto Lilienthal's 1894 glider and Wiley Post's *Winnie Mae,* a Lockheed Vega 5C; Post twice flew it around the

When Pan American wanted to reconnoiter the possibilities for international routes across the Pacific, they called on Charles Lindbergh to do the job. He and his wife, Anne Morrow, flew this Lockheed Sirius to Alaska, the coast of Siberia, Japan, and China, and on a 30,000-mile tour to Europe and South America. The Sirius design is one of several variants of the famous Vega. Pan Am could not use the research of the Lindberghs to establish their Trans Pacific routes, since they were unable to obtain permission from Japan and the Soviet Union for the bases they needed. Instead, they developed a route to Manila via Midway, Wake, and Guam Island. The name *Tingmissartoq,* painted forward of the cockpit, comes from the Eskimo for "The one who flies like a big bird." It is part of the National Air and Space Museum collection.

The National Air and Space Museum has the most representative collection of aviation artifacts anywhere, and many of the items on display are of great interest to antiquers. Four of the aircraft in this picture are historically connected. The Ford Trimotor of the late twenties (top) was doomed to obsolescence when the first of the modern airliners, the Boeing 247

(lower left), appeared in 1933. The 247, in turn, was marked for extinction when the DC-1 first flew only six months later. The DC-1 was the prototype for the DC-2, from which the DC-3 (middle left) was developed. To its right is a Northrop Alpha. The innovative wing and superstructure techniques used in the Alpha were adapted for use in the DC-1, -2, and -3.

world. General Billy Mitchell's Spad XVI and Calbraith P. Rodgers's *Vin Fiz*, a Wright biplane, are there. The *Vin Fiz* made the first coast-to-coast flight.

Lindbergh, by the way, made several visits to the original Smithsonian building to see his *Spirit of St. Louis*. He once asked for a private showing of the airplane. Using a ladder, he climbed into the cockpit and sat there silently for some forty minutes.

Aircraft of interest to antiquers:

1928 Lockheed Vega 5 of Amelia Earhart
1929 Fairchild FC-2
1929 Lockheed 8 Sirius of Charles and Anne Morrow Lindbergh
1929 Waco 9 of Marion McClure
1930 Lockheed 5C Vega *Winnie Mae* of Wiley Post

1930 Pitcairn PA-5 Mailwing
1936 Turner RT-14 Meteor
1936 Buecker BU133 Jungmeister
1937 Hughes H-1 (which broke the transcontinental speed record)

FLORIDA · Pensacola · Naval Aviation Museum

This museum should be high on the list of "musts" for those fascinated by aviation's earliest days. Although the emphasis here is of course primarily military, the breadth of the collection—from Pusher to jet—is outstanding. Several of the aircraft types on display are like those restored by individual antiquers, such as the primary trainers of the World War II era.

The 1917 Curtiss NC-4 is of special historical interest, since it was the first aircraft to successfully complete a transatlantic crossing. The saga of the crossing attempt by this ship and its two sister craft makes fascinating reading.

The museum also has one of the last surviving Ford Trimotors.

Nearly 100 aircraft
Aircraft of interest to antiquers:

1911 Curtiss A-1 replica
1917 Curtiss NC-4
Jenny

Ford Trimotor
Primary trainers of World War II vintage

ILLINOIS · Chicago · Museum of Science and Industry

Even though there are only six aircraft in this enormous collection of man's technological artifacts, any antiquer will enjoy a visit to Chicago's Museum of Science and Industry. The displays of processes and products are without parallel in the Western world.

Six aircraft
Aircraft of interest to antiquers:

1910 Curtiss Pusher   1917 Curtiss JN-4D Jenny

IOWA · Blakesburg · Airpower Museum

This museum is closely associated with the Antique Airplane Association in spirit, if not on paper. It is located at Antique Airfield, the headquarters of the association and the scene of the antique movement's biggest fly-ins.

The museum has several aircraft undergoing restoration, most of which are types that have been restored at one time or another by individual antiquers. As such, it is an excellent source of information on restoration. It has a collection of many maintenance manuals and other similar materials that can help an antiquer to bring his machine back to life.

Future plans include some changes in the static display material and the opening of an extensive library, for which a new facility has been constructed.

Twenty aircraft
Aircraft of interest to antiquers:

1929 Fairchild 71   1931 Stinson Junior
1930 Monocoupe Model 91   1937 Arrow Sport

MICHIGAN · Dearborn · Henry Ford Museum

Another "must" for antiquers. Its collection consists entirely of civilian aircraft, reflecting Henry Ford's antimilitaristic sentiments, and has examples that are both exceptionally rare and of outstanding historical value.

It has the only Fokker Trimotor on display in the United States. This was one of the first aircraft to make flying acceptable to passengers and was in part the inspiration for the Ford Trimotor.

Naturally, an example of the Ford Trimotor is part of the collection. Each of the two Trimotors was used by Admiral Byrd for polar exploration. The Fokker went to the Arctic and the Ford to the Antarctic.

In addition to these three-engine historical gems, the museum contains the 1939 VS-300, Sikorsky's first successful helicopter and the realization of his lifelong dream, also the first helicopter to fly in the United States; a 1910 Blériot; a 1929 Vega, and a 1931 Pitcairn PCA2 Autogiro.

Ford, who hated flying and flew only once (with Lindbergh on a short hop), made some tremendous contributions to aviation history. Basically, he tried to make the benefits of flying available to the general public. He attempted to apply his mass-production methods to airliners, and his was the first systematic effort to make airplanes congenial to the public with a civilized terminal building, scheduled flights, provisions for mail transport, and so on. Furthermore, he organized the Ford Air Tours, competitions that criss-crossed the country each year from 1925 to 1931. The tours were designed to make the public more aviation conscious.

Twenty aircraft
Aircraft of interest to antiquers:

1910 Blériot	1931 Pitcairn Autogiro
1926 Fokker VII (Trimotor)	1939 Vought-Sikorsky VS-300
1928 Ford Trimotor	helicopter —the first successful
1929 Lockheed Vega	U.S. helicopter design

NEBRASKA · Minden · Harold Warp Pioneer Village

Although the emphasis at this museum is almost exclusively on cars, the collection does contain a 1929 Cessna Model A, which is quite a rare machine. It is one of Clyde Cessna's earliest attempts to apply his monoplane design philosophy to the lightplane market.

Thirteen aircraft, emphasis on cars
Aircraft of interest to antiquers:

1903 Wright *Flyer* replica	1929 Cessna Model A
1910 Curtiss Pusher	

NEVADA · Reno · Harrah's Automobile Collection

As the name implies, the collection in this museum is made up practically entirely of automobiles. However, Harrah's does have a Jenny and one of the few Ford Trimotors left.

Twelve aircraft, five on display
Aircraft of interest to antiquers:

1918 Curtis JN-4D Jenny   1937 Arrow Sport Model F
1928 Ford Trimotor

NEW MEXICO · Santa Fe · Wings of Yesterday Flying Air Museum

Dave Allyn's Wings of Yesterday is the culmination of his lifelong dream of having a collection of active, flying antiques presented for public appreciation, both on the ground and in the air. Dave tries to have at least one of the aircraft make a demonstration flight each week—and in the problem-free weather of New Mexico, this is a realistic goal.

The museum is particularly convenient, compared to many others, since it is located on the grounds of a major airport. On a cross-country trip, it should be within reason for many antiquers to stop in and pay Dave a visit.

Fourteen aircraft, twelve on display
Aircraft of interest to antiquers:

1918 Fokker D7
1928 Crosley Moonbeam biplane
1931 Waco RNF   1935 American Eaglet
1931 Stinson SM-6000B Trimotor   1935 Navy N3N biplane trainer
  (sole airworthy example)   1938 Lockheed Electra Jr. 12A

NEW YORK · Hammondsport · Glenn H. Curtiss Museum of Local History

Of the earliest aviation pioneers, including the Wrights, Glenn Curtiss had the most impact on the technological progress made during aviation's earliest

This Curtiss June Bug replica is now in the Glenn H. Curtiss Museum of Local History in Hammondsport, New York. It is a masterpiece of painstaking reconstruction. In addition to this aircraft and a Pusher, mentioned on page 167, this charming museum has a 1918 Curtiss JN-4 Jenny, almost all variations of the Curtiss OX-5 engine, a 1929 Mercury Chick, and a 1927 Curtiss Robin. Hammondsport is in the beautiful Finger Lakes district of New York State. It is also not far from Elmira, New York (the closest commercial air service), home of Schweizer sailplane makers and the National Soaring Museum.

beginnings. This was because, in contrast to the many dreamer/designers, Curtiss was not just an engineer but also a businessman. He was able to take the technological advances he made and shape them into items he could sell. He was such a good marketer, in fact, that he would often create a market for his goods.

For example, he was not the first to realize that a military contract for aircraft could mean a lot of money, but he did go to the extreme of training military men for free, knowing they would need aircraft to fly and would also promote the idea of flying. This was at a time when there were no military pilots.

This fascinating museum contains evidence that shows what a genius Curtiss was and how far, technologically speaking, he traveled from the most primitive days of powered flight to his relatively sophisticated machines of two decades later.

Curtiss was originally drawn into aviation not because of any success with airframe design but because he had a fabulous record as a maker of motorcycle engines which, of course, had to be light yet powerful—desirable qualities in aircraft powerplants.

The progression of these powerplants is shown at the museum, from motorcycles to post–World War I aviation designs. Several antiques in the movement use Curtiss engines, including the OX-5 and its variants and the Challenger.

The museum is located in a former schoolhouse in Curtiss's charming hometown, which is situated in the vineyard country of New York State. A pilgrimage to this museum is well worth the effort for an antiquer.

Nine aircraft
Aircraft of interest to antiquers:

1911 Curtiss Pusher
1918 Curtiss JN-4
1919 Curtiss Oriole

1927 Curtiss Robin
1929 Mercury Chick

NEW YORK · Rhinebeck · Old Rhinebeck Aerodrome

This collection of antique aircraft replicas is not a museum in the strictest sense but is more a representation of a passion. The passion belongs to Cole Palen and is shared by his many friends who delight in servicing the most difficult of aviation's creations in order to keep them flying.

Hudson Valley skies are torn each summer weekend by the sputtering and roaring of old radials, rotaries, and other small engines, which power machines that only a few pilots are qualified—or would dare—to fly. Palen, Dave Fox, and others fly them for their own enjoyment as well as for that of the hundreds of visitors who flock to this famous airstrip all summer long.

Palen's collection and airshow are unique in the United States. No one else has seen fit to make these cantankerous machines their life's work, with the possible exception of the folks at the Shuttleworth Trust collection of early flying machines in Old Warden, England.

Fifty-one aircraft, twenty-nine airworthy and all of interest to antiquers
Aircraft of special interest to antiquers:

1909 Voisin

1910 Short S-29

1918 Fokker D7

1918 Spad XIII

This Blériot is just about the oldest airworthy antique aircraft in the United States. It is part of Cole Palen's collection. It does more hopping than real flying. It takes a very brave person to fly the Blériot; its controllability is marginal in no-wind conditions and not even worth risking when the breezes blow. The Blériot pictured here is an authentic relic of the earliest days of powered flight but was probably not built in France. Its precise origins are unknown, but more than likely it is a copy, and was not necessarily built with the permission of the original designer—a common practice in the pioneering days of aviation history. Note that there are no ailerons on the wing; the pilot warps the airfoil by a set of wire controls instead.

Revving up the rotary on a Deperdussin replica, a part of the Cole Palen collection. Palen is one of the few persons in the world who has the patience and devotion to fool with the highly temperamental designs of aviation's earliest days. These planes are so fragile, so painstaking to reconstruct, and so marginally airworthy that they are hardly ever flown. More usually, they are "hopped" down a grass runway such as this, because even the slightest breeze can result in disaster. In spite of all this, they have their very own intriguing appeal, just like their sister ships of a few years later, and Palen never lacks for volunteers eager to help. The spiral-lath buildup of the monocoque fuselage is visible here. The Deperdussin used wing warping.

OHIO · Cleveland · Frederick C. Crawford Auto-Aviation Museum

To an antiquer, Cleveland means air races. The Cleveland Air Races were held during the golden age of aviation's development, and many of the machines flying in the antique movement today are either derivations of those machines or types that actually competed.

One of the most sought-after prizes in the late thirties was the Thompson Trophy, which is now housed in this museum.

The museum also has an example of a 1917 flying boat. Curtiss was fascinated with the idea of water-flying, from the time of his earliest involvement with aircraft development. He was among the first to realize that by designing a "step" into his hulls and floats, he would be able to overcome the suction that kept his machines from leaving the water.

Six aircraft
Note: Houses the Thompson Air Race Trophy
Aircraft of interest to antiquers:

1910 Curtiss Pusher
1917 Thomas Morse Scout
1917 Curtiss flying boat

1920 Curtiss Oriole
1931 Wedell-Williams Special

OHIO · Dayton · The Air Force Museum

This museum has an enormous collection of aircraft, most of which, naturally, are military and of historical interest. There are, however, examples of many trainers of World War I and II vintage such as have been restored in substantial numbers and form part of the hard core of the antique movement.

In addition, there is a portion of the museum devoted to Dayton's first two citizens who made their name in aviation, the Wright brothers.

It is interesting to note that the main exhibition hall of this museum was paid for not by government dollars collected from taxpayers but by contributions direct from the public.

Over 100 aircraft
Aircraft of interest to antiquers:

1911 Wright Model B
  (highly modified)
1916–19 vintage Curtiss JN-4D
  Jenny
1917–18 vintage Camel replica

1917–18 vintage Standard J-1
  (partial aircraft)
1918 Standard E-1
1942 Piper L-4
1942 Stinson L-5

This unique amphibian was built in 1931 by the Budd Company, which made its name producing streamline trains, not airplaines. According to the sign beneath the aircraft, Budd built this tiny aircraft, which has a fuselage about the size of a canoe, "to demonstrate the practicability of its 'shotweld' process of fabricating stainless steel, subsequently employed by the Budd Co. in building lightweight railroad trains." The aircraft, which was called *The Pioneer,* was flown approximately 1000 hours in the United States and Europe. Strangely enough, this was not the only stainless-steel amphib built. The Fleetwing Seabird had a spot-welded stainless-steel hull and represented a very interesting solution to the problems associated with flying off the water. Both the prototype, designated F-401, and one of the five production versions, called F-5s, survive.

OHIO · Port Clinton · Island Airlines

Aircraft of interest to antiquers:

Until recently the last scheduled regular operation of a Ford Trimotor, from Port Clinton to Put-in-Bay on South Bass Island. Its Ford, a 4-AT-B, was damaged in a mishap but is being rebuilt.

OKLAHOMA · Muskogee · Antiques, Inc.

Six aircraft
Aircraft of interest to antiquers:

Nieuport fighter of World War I   Fairchild KR-21 trainer
Fokker Triplane of World War I

PENNSYLVANIA · Philadelphia · The Franklin Institute Science Museum

Six aircraft
Only permanent exhibit of a 707 in the world, a gift of British Airways. Visitors may examine both the inside and the outside of this machine, which is itself becoming somewhat of an antique in the world of air transport. Aircraft of interest to antiquers:

1911 Wright Model B   1931 Budd stainless steel
                                         amphibian—one of a kind

PENNSYLVANIA · Toughkenamon · Colonial Flying Corps Museum

Ten aircraft, mostly flyable
Aircraft of interest to antiquers:

1937 Fairchild 24G   1940 DeHavilland D.H.82
  (a popular restoration)   Tiger Moth

VIRGINIA · Bealton · Flying Circus Aerodrome

This is not strictly a museum per se but more a collection of antique aircraft used for air shows on weekends from May to October. The air shows include World War I dogfights, fly-bys of golden age aircraft, hot-air balloons, and flying comedy acts.

Twenty-two aircraft
Aircraft of interest to antiquers:

Sopwith Pup   Waco UPF-7
1930 Fleet 1   Stearman PT-17
1931 DeHavilland Tiger Moth

VIRGINIA · Fredricksburg · Shannon Air Museum

Plenty here for the antiquer to see. The 1914 Standard is rotary powered and very rare but not as rare as the Spad, which is the only one of these famous World War I fighters still airworthy. The best time to come to this museum is during a summer fly-in when some of these machines are actually flown.

The Mailwing is also rare—few survive of the thirty built. The Aeronca C-2 had a real impact on the general-aviation scene in spite of a strange shape that earned it the sobriquet "flying bathtub." It and its derivative, the C-3, were extremely popular fun-flying machines during the early thirties.

This monoplane has one of the earliest horizontally opposed engines, and its wings are braced with wires top and bottom. Of the 112 built, this and one other are the only airworthy examples.

Six aircraft
Aircraft of interest to antiquers:

1914 Standard E-1   1932 Aeronca C-2 Deluxe Scout
1916 Spad VII   1932 Vultee V-1A
1927 Pitcairn PA-5 Mailwing   1938 Stinson Reliant
1927 Travel Air 2000   1945 Piper J-3 Cub
1929 Curtiss-Robertson J-1 Robin

WISCONSIN • Franklin (suburb of Milwaukee) • Paul H. Poberezny Museum (formerly the Experimental Aircraft Association Museum)

The EAA museum covers all of sport aviation's facets, including antiquing. Not only does it have a fascinating assemblage of old aircraft but several in different stages of restoration. This allows a restorer to examine closely the structure of representative old aircraft and examples of what has been done to make them sound enough to fly again.

Next to the Jenny is an SE-5—the famous British World War I fighter— also without its fabric skin. Then there's the Rearwin fuselage, wings, and engine, cleaned and primed but without fabric—a good chance to examine metal-tube construction.

The majority of the EAA's members are homebuilders, and therefore most of the floor space in the museum is devoted to homebuilt aircraft. Of interest to the antiquer are the displays of different construction methods and repaint techniques—even on antiques. There is a Travel Air 4000 vertical stabilizer, which has had a rather complicated corner replaced in part. It has a good example of a wood splice—a small new piece that blends perfectly into the aged framework of the stabilizer.

A visit to the shops in the rear of the building turns up two antiques being restored among the numerous homebuilt projects. One is a Waco UPF-7 with special historical significance, and the other is the first Travel Air.

Here again are examples of restorations actually under way, being accomplished by skilled craftsmen who also happen to be very friendly EAA members.

The museum also contains an excellent group of early aircraft engines that represent aviation powerplant development in the first decades of aeronautical history. Some of these are displayed in cutaway form, like the training models used in aircraft mechanic schools.

Finally, there is a collection of antique props, and a sequential display of a wooden prop in various stages from wooden block to finished product.

One hundred fifty in collection, about ninety on display
Aircraft of interest to antiquers:

1912 Curtiss Pusher   SE-5
Curtiss JN-4 Jenny

The Monocoupe is one of the more popular antique restorations. This 1935 Model 90A, part of the EAA collection, was donated by Richard Wagner of Lyons, Wisconsin.

With its Duralumin monocoque construction, this 1936 Luscombe was a standard setter for the lightplane industry. Only twenty-two of these ships were manufactured, but they were models of efficiency. With a 145-hp Warner SS-50A engine, they cruised at 142 mph. This example has been loaned by George Ramin, of Houston, Texas, to the EAA Museum.

CANADA · Ontario · Ottawa · National Aeronautical Collection

One of the world's best aviation collections, due in no small part to some strong government support.

Ninety-five aircraft, usually 39 on display
Aircraft of interest to antiquers:

1911 Blériot XI
1917 Curtiss JN-4 (Can.)
   (Canadian-manufactured design
   based on the Jenny, but with
   improvements)
1921 Curtiss Seagull (used for
   exploration in Brazil, 1924–25)
1928 DeHavilland 60 Cirrus Moth

1928 Fairchild FC2-W2
1929 Bellanca Pacemaker 1929
ca. 1930 A. E. A. Silver Dart (two
   replicas based on the 1909 design
   Aeronca C-2)
1932 Junkers W-34
1940 Fleet Finch

CANADA · Alberta · Wetaskiwin · Reynolds Museum

Six aircraft in collection, three on display
Aircraft of interest to antiquers:

1917 Curtiss JN-4D
1924 DeHavilland Cirrus

1926 DeHavilland Gypsy Moth
1932 Pietenpol monoplane

The first task is to find someone who is an IA in your area. An IA is a person who has an Inspector's Authorization from the FAA, which allows him to inspect and sign off in the aircraft's records any kind of repairs. He is usually referred to as the authorized inspector. He must have his A & P license before he may be designated an inspector.

Generally, there is an IA in every general-aviation repair shop; if there isn't, the shop will know where the nearest one is. He is often a mechanic who has his own repair facility at an airport. The trick is to find one who is experienced or qualified to inspect an antique. This can be difficult, but not impossible.

An antiquer planning to do a restoration would be well advised to get together with the IA at the outset, right when the antique is purchased. If the antique is airworthy, the IA will want to do an annual inspection; if it is a basketcase, he will want to look at the parts in your basket, since sooner or later he will be inspecting their condition and the way you put them together. He may even be able to give you tips on how to go about it.

More than one aircraft has been built up entirely around its data plate. This is the little metal plate where the Aircraft Type Certificate number, serial number, and a few other statistics have been stamped to give your machine an identity it will never lose. Precedent means a lot in the world of aviation officialdom, and this is *the* precedent most important on an antique.

Another helpful precedent is the N number—the registration number—of the aircraft. Even when the aircraft is a basketcase, if the owner can find out the original N number and it has not been issued to another aircraft, he will be able to get a copy of the original Airworthiness Certificate for that particular aircraft from the files of the FAA in Oklahoma City (see address on page 246).

Not only that: if you have the N number, you can get copies of all the Form 337s for your antique. This form describes major repairs and alterations that have been done to your machine. The IA will be interested in these because he will want to inspect the quality of the work to see if it has withstood the test of time.

He may also find evidence of AD note* compliance there, although he is more likely to look for it in the logbooks for the aircraft. There may be logbooks for the engine, the airframe, and the propeller. A concerted effort should be made to acquire these and any other records at the time of purchase.

Compliance with ADs—mandatory design modifications issued by the government—is a very important item. The IA will not sign off the aircraft as airworthy unless all the ADs for the particular type have been accomplished to his satisfaction.

The necessity of "going by the book" in aircraft repair work cannot be overstressed. In this case, of course, "the book" is made up of Federal Air Regulations,

---

*AD notes or Airworthiness Directives are issued by the FAA when a problem shows up that appears to relate to the design of an aircraft. They may be changes in control surfaces, fairings, etc., that affect the flying characteristics of the aircraft, modifications to spars to make them stronger, and so on.

called FARs for short. The FARs are broken down into divisions referred to as parts. For example, Part 21 explains the ATC, or Aircraft Type Certificate, which is what an aircraft gets when it is certified by the government for manufacture.

The necessity of doing repair work in accordance with established procedure is described in FAR Part 43. The limitations on N-number markings are described in FAR Part 45. If an aircraft is old enough, one may use the original "NC" style of markings—big numbers on the wings and little numbers on the tail—to add a touch of authenticity.

FAR Part 47 describes what is necessary to re-register your aircraft if it has been out of registration for a while.

Most important of all to the antiquer doing a lot of his or her own work is familiarization with FAR Part 65. This section discusses the roles of the owner/pilot, the A & P, and the IA—what the limitations are of each on the kind of work they can do to an aircraft. Appendix A of Part 65 is the one that tells about the pilot/owner's role.

Antiquers may grumble about the constrictions imposed by the FARs, but compared to other countries, at least the *possibility* of restoring an aircraft remains quite open in the United States. Other countries sometimes have so much red tape to overcome that an antiquer will give up in disgust. An avid buff ends up doing his antiquing from an armchair with an aviation magazine in his hands—a far cry from actually experiencing the majesty of an antique in flight.

Where to write to obtain copies of the records on your aircraft.

Airman and Aircraft Registry
Federal Aviation Agency
P.O. Box 25082
Oklahoma City, Oklahoma 73125

BIBLIOGRAPHY

Allen, Richard Sanders. *Revolution in the Sky*. Brattleboro, Vt.: Stephen Greene Press, 1967.

Bowers, Peter M. *Antique Plane Guide*. Modern Aircraft Series. New York: Crown Publishers, 1962.

Carpenter, Dorr B., and Mayborn, Mitch. *Ryan Guidebook*. Dallas: Flying Enterprise Publications, 1975.

Dwiggins, Don. *Restoration of Antique and Classic Planes*. Modern Aircraft Series. New York: Crown Publishers, 1975.

Federal Aviation Administration. *Acceptable Methods, Techniques and Practices. Aircraft Inspection and Repair*. Washington, D.C.: U.S. Government Printing Office, 1973.

————— *Personal Aircraft Inspection Handbook*. Washington, D.C.: U.S. Government Printing Office, 1964.

Ingells, Douglas J. *Tin Goose*. Fallbrook, California: Aero Publishers, 1968.

Matt, Paul R. *Benny Howard and His DGA Racers*. All-American Collectors Series, vol. 14, part 3. Glendale, California: Aviation Book Co., 1975.

Mayborn, Mitch, and Bowers, Peter M. *Stearman Guidebook*. Dallas: Flying Enterprise Publications, 1973.

Rice, M. S. *Guide to Pre-1930 Aircraft Engines*. Appleton, Wisconsin: Graphic Communications Center, 1972.

Shamburger, Page. *Classic Monoplanes*. Modern Aircraft Series. New York: Crown Publishers, 1966.

Smith, Robert T. *Classic Biplanes*. Modern Aircraft Series. New York: Crown Publishers, 1968.

Spencer, Ruth. *Aircraft Woodwork*. Modern Aircraft Series. New York: Crown Publishers, 1972.

—————, and Spencer, Warren. *Aircraft Dope and Fabric*. Modern Aircraft Series. New York: Crown Publishers, 1970.

Underwood, John W. *Of Monocoupes and Men*. Glendale, California: Aviation Book Company, 1973.

Page references in *italics* indicate captions.